A RESTLESS LIFE

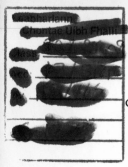

First published in 2008 by
Liberties Press
Guinness Enterprise Centre | Taylor's Lane | Dublin 8 | Ireland
www.libertiespress .com
info@libertiespress.com
+353 (1) 415 1224

Trade enquiries to CMD Distribution
55A Spruce Avenue | Stillorgan Industrial Park | Blackrock | County Dublin
Tel: +353 (1) 294 2560
Fax: +353 (1) 294 2564

Distributed in the United States by
DuFour Editions | PO Box 7 | Chester Springs | Pennsylvania | 19425
and in Australia by
InBooks | 3 Narabang Way | Belrose NSW 2085

Copyright © Leland Bardwell, 2008

The author has asserted her moral rights.

Hardback: ISBN: 978–1–905483–46–4
Paperback: ISBN: 978–1–905483–52–5

2 4 6 8 10 9 7 5 3 1

A CIP record for this title is available from the British Library.

Liberties Press gratefully acknowledges the financial assistance of the
Arts Council in relation to the publication of this title.

Cover design by Liam Furlong at space.ie
Internal design by Liberties Press
Set in Garamond
Printed by CPD

A RESTLESS LIFE

LELAND BARDWELL

In memory of
Pat and Mary Hone

ACKNOWLEDGEMENTS

The poem 'Lobster Fishing' (pages 274–75) originally appeared in *The Noise of Masonry Settling* (Dedalus, 2006). 'Lines to My Father' (pages 62–63) was first published in *Arena* magazine.

CONTENTS

Nothing I write is as true as my fiction.

NADINE GORDIMER

Tell all the truth but at a slant.

EMILY DICKINSON

If I hadn't been a writer I'd have been a good housewife.

ANAÏS NIN

PROLOGUE

We were all born under cabbages then. Or found. So I chose mine. I chose mine because it was broad and leafy – one of the biggest in the row of cabbages in my grandfather's garden. There was some argument about this, I remember, but I stuck to my guns. It reminded me of a clocking hen the way it sat squat on the ground. This garden ended in the apex of a falling triangle on Kilmore Hill and we could slide in through the wrought-iron bars of the gate without being seen.

The hill was bordered with fuchsia, and below, Killiney Bay, as glorious as the Bay of Naples, stretched away to Bray Head, the slopes a profusion of eucalyptus and hebe, interspersed with palm trees, waving their semaphore leaves. And here I met my sister, Paloma, for the first time. She was squinting into the sun and she was wearing a salmon-pink dress made of silk. At two and a half and demented, I fell in love with her. Malarian and yellow with incipient jaundice, I followed her wherever she went. Whatever she did, I copied. I clung to her like a burr. When she tried to pick me off, I bawled. In the thin east wind, we paddled in the sea, pebbles bruising our insteps, our sandshoes tucked under our arms.

And that was when I met my grandparents: my grandfather with stubble on his chin like wood shavings, who wore his glasses on his forehead and was always in a hurry, my grandmother, severe and ponderous, dressed in black. Always black. The materials black and shiny as oil. Her dress, or dresses, hung straight to the ground and she was permanently displeased.

These facts, however, were remote from me in my third year. Playing tig with my sister's love kept me in a state of tension. She loves me, she loves me not, says the dandelion clock.

But the steamer trunks had not yet been unpacked for good. That winter we returned to India.

PART I

A Child in India – Coming and Going

The liner is riding gracefully up the Red Sea towards the Suez Canal. The child is restless. She noses her way out of the cabin, climbs the deck stairs and totters to the edge of the deck. She looks forward to the party. The ship's cook is making tarts for her and she will wear the organdie dress. The Queen of Hearts will have some tarts all on a summer's day.

The child's mother is wearing a tussore dress that hangs straight down to the calves of her legs. Her blonde hair is tied behind her head in a bun. Today she wears flat, strapped shoes.

She sees the child near the edge of the deck and she feels her anger spiralling up through her chest. She picks up the child and rushes her into the cabin. She tells the child: if she is naughty like that again she will tell Grandma. The child has been told over and over again not to leave the cabin or go near the deck alone, and since the child never listens to what the mother says there is only one thing to do: forbid the child to go to the party. She may not wear the organdie dress with the red paper hearts. She will not be the Queen of Hearts ever again.

The tussore is cool against the child's cheek as she is carried under the mother's arm. In the cabin, the mother lays the child on the berth. She goes out and closes the door.

The child dreams. She is in the bungalow at Perambhur. A lion leaps out of the shadows. The child runs from room to room, the lion pads after her. Where is her Ayah? Her Ayah guards her from all wild animals. She runs to her Ayah and burrows into her. The lion is afraid and goes away.

The child's father carries a gun under his arm. He carries it loosely as he would a newspaper. He has heard there is a hyena in the neighbourhood. The father wears a light, khaki-coloured jacket, trousers tucked into leggings. He doesn't wear a topi, as she must, only a soft-brimmed felt hat. The child toddles after the father, calls 'Daddy, Daddy'. There is only herself and her father. He does not find the hyena.

The child runs out of the bungalow. She finds the hose and squirts water all over herself. The water splashes and gurgles; her sodden dress is glued to her body. She has never been so happy, so cool, so alone. Her mother runs out. 'I have told you time and time again never to go out without your topi. You never listen.' The child never listens. The mother pulls the wet clothes off the child as she drags her into the house.

The stables go on fire. Everyone runs. Everyone shouts. The two horses will be burnt. The Seiss (horse's groom) runs into the stables and drags the horses out. The Seiss is very brave. His loose shirt is scorched. The mother rubs salve into his arms. He does not cry out. The horses are safe. One of them is white.

The child's father makes railways. He works on the Madras Southern and Midland Railway. The child spells 'railways': M. S. and M. He is responsible for bridges. He looks bored in his office. He chews his pencil.

The child learns railway words: sidings, points, cow-catchers, buffers, couplings, sleepers, tenders.

The family is riding on the trolley. Two Indians push the trolley. They run along the rails. They are barefoot and wear only a loincloth. The mother and the child face the Indians. The father stands forward, holding the tiller. They come to a bridge. The Indians jump off and run through the tunnel. A train is due.

They run back and lift the trolley off the rails. The train passes. The trolley is put back on the rails. The mother says 'Look, look'. Above them on a hill, some women are doing their *dobhi* (laundry) . A herd of elephants comes and scatters the washing. The women run screaming in all directions. 'Isn't it amazing,' the mother says.

The mother gets off the ship at Port Said. They will be here for some time. The child waits on the ship for her mother's return. The mother will buy her a bangle if she is good. When her mother returns to the ship, she has a beaded bag with jewellery in it. Her father also carries a parcel.

'Pat, look,' her mother says to her father. She holds up an amethyst snake with diamond eyes. She puts it round her neck. Her father holds her mother by the two shoulders. 'It suits you, Mary,' he says. He then undoes his own parcel and lifts out a salmon-pink silk dress. 'It will look lovely on Paloma,' he says.

The child waits patiently for her bangle. She holds out her podgy arm. 'Another time,' her mother says. The snake bounces on her mother's neck as she is dragged into the cabin.

'No, mummy, no!'

'I won't have this behaviour.'

Ireland is gone again. The crickets sing in the hot Indian nights. She is the youngest now of three. The storm lantern hangs from a hook on the veranda. It casts a blue glow on the wooden wall. The child and her brother are learning the present tense of the Latin verb 'to love'. They tell her Paloma is delicate and need not do lessons every day. The child says '*Amo, amas amat, amamus, amatis, amant.*' 'Now,' Aiyuni says, 'I want you to say it, Noll.' The child interrupts again. '*Amo, amas.*' 'Keep quiet,' Aiyuni says. The child says sorry and the brother begins again. Aiyuni has brought Noll and Paloma out to India to 'learn the Latin', as they are missing school.

Aiyuni Cooper has red hair which she wears in coils each side of her head like telephones. The child trails after her cousin, Aiyuni. She loves her. Aiyuni says she is tired and wants to be left alone. Sometimes she cries because she is lonely. She says the child is very willful and must not show off. The child promises in future not to do it any more.

The family is on the beach at Madras. There is another family, the Wilkinsons. They are also Irish, and Pat Wilkinson works on the railways. Sally Wilkinson is the child's godmother. She is Jewish. Their daughter, Deirdre, is older than the child, and their son, Harry, is the same age.

Noll and Paloma are making sandcastles. The child wades into the sea and her camiknickers balloon out in the water. They get waterlogged and straps drag at her shoulders. She pees in the warm water. It is fun to pee where no one can see. She wants to stay in the water all day.

They are going on a picnic. The whole family. All the Hones and the Wilkinsons. They walk through fields. Her mother brings her sketch pad. They come to a gate. The child runs in front and climbs the gate into the next field. The party follows her. Then the bisons come. They gallop towards the party, scatter the baskets. Everybody is angry. 'Very very angry,' her mother says. It is all the child's fault. The picnic is spoilt.

The ship sails majestically away from Port Said. Leaving the Suez Canal, it ploughs into the Mediterranean. The child is in the cabin with her mother.

'Time for your cascara,' the mother says.

She turns her head away. She shuts her mouth tight.

'Open your mouth.'

'No.'

'If you don't open your mouth, I'll tell Grandma.'

16

The child takes in the cascara and spits it out into the basin.

The mother takes down the child's knickers. She puts her over her knee and brings out the cane.

The child is a little mongoose that runs up and down a stick. She is the great slayer of snakes and rats. She will be loved because she kills all dangerous beasts and reptiles. Everyone will say 'Ah, here comes the wonderful mongoose'.

The child wants to go home to her Ayah. She has malaria and jaundice. She lies in her cot under the mosquito net. Her Ayah is in the mist beyond the net. Today she is wearing her brown sari. She smiles. Her large body is wound up like a tub. An uncle enters the room. He looks at her. Laughs. He calls her 'Yaller'.

The ship lands and they are on the gangway. Everyone is leaving the ship. Porters run up and down, scaling and jumping the railings. Cabin trunks are being lifted out of the hold. The mother holds the child's hand but the child tries to wriggle away. The mother has a leather attaché case in her other hand. Her father is walking behind with a cricket bat under his arm. He sniffs the new cool air. Her aunt waits at the foot of the gangway.

The Red Sea and the Suez Canal were folded away. The square bungalow on the hill in Perambhur. The wide Indian plains. The paddy fields. The heat. My much-loved Ayah. They were all eclipsed by the new *now* of a castellated house at the end of Killiney beach, called Dunmara. In the top tower, with its pretence at antiquity, lived Aiyuni. I was four and a half — my brother was at a prep school in Bray — and Paloma and I did our lessons with Aiyuni from nine to twelve every day.

I soon forgot the past. I now had Paloma all to myself. I arranged our games with military precision. But when she was clever enough to get rid of me, I'd roam the beach alone, climbing on the outcrop of rock, collecting pebbles, shells of every colour, sea urchins, the discarded sheaths of razor fish. My two-year-old excitement of that summer in my grandfather's garden at the foot of Kilmore Hill, where I first met my sister and where the raspberries turned pale in your plate of cream, where the peas were as soft as Indian silk, and where the garden smelled of parsley, mint and fresh-dug earth, had prepared me well for this new Irish existence. Although now it was cold, the sand grey and wet, the sea darkening at four o'clock. My mother would call and call, and I, lost in my wanderings, would pretend not to hear, my treasures safe in my bathing cap. 'Dirty, dirty,' she'd say, and empty them out on the sand.

One day, I hit upon an idea. The cook, maid, cleaner, old as a tree, never used the lavatory. Instead she'd go outside the back door, open her legs under her voluminous skirts and pee like a mare. Let's pee in the pie dishes, I suggested to Paloma. Paloma, who wasn't naughty like I was, nevertheless fell in with my idea. The enamel pie dishes were stacked outside the larder in a pyramid. It was the day after my fifth birthday, and I was full of fun.

We arranged the pie dishes in a row and carefully peed in each one, and ran to hide under a box hedge. Oh, sweet terror – calls, dogs barking, cold wind, suppressed giggles. The wish for death. That night, a family conference was held. Someone said, 'She was so good on her birthday.'

While my grandfather travelled the train every day – the train that swayed through the tunnel, the far side of Killiney Station to skirt the Vico Road and beyond through Dalkey and Blackrock, bringing the white-collared workers to the city – my mother pined for a wider life.

She was not happy in this pseudo-castle, with nothing to do only tend the garden. All through the First World War, she had courted and married Pat Hone. Every day they corresponded, hundreds of letters coming from the trenches.

Dearest Mary . . . I'm sending you a little lace kerchief made here. I think it's nice. They make good lace hereabouts.

Dearest Mary . . . saying that he believed I was a good fellow and that I had played rugby football for Ireland. He would get a shock if he saw me playing rugby footfall.

My Dearest . . . We have been working under the most miserable conditions imaginable, rain and all damnation, no moon, utter beastliness . . . I should willingly give all the money I have for the war to be over.

8th June 1915
Dearest Mary, We are out of the trenches today. Less rats. The view reminds me of Killiney. I hope your headache is better.

What must she have written to him? None of her letters survive. But he, working before the war on the Canadian Pacific Railway, joined the 2nd Canadian Division Signallers. Like many another Irishman, he was drawn into this conflagration, which he described in one of his letters.

You can't have war and common sense. Fighting for 'right' has no meaning any more.

He survived. He was a brave man. He was awarded the Military Cross for saving a man from being gassed. But he never spoke of the war afterwards. How could he?

So, with a wife and two children, he had had no choice but to go abroad again. For an engineer in Ireland then, there was little or no work, hence his going to India, taking his pregnant wife with him and leaving the two eldest with his sister, Olive.

But at home in Ireland now, for good, my mother looked on this house in Killiney as a mere stepping stone to a more permanent residence, a place where she could expand away from her own family and that of the Hones.

Pat Hone was born in 35 Lower Leeson Street, Dublin, had been pushed in his high pram round St Stephen's Green, growing up with his elder brother, Joe, his elder sister, Olive, and his younger brother, Kit. Because of his mother's having died young, Olive took it upon herself to bring up the younger ones – three pretty boys in sailor suits.

There was a noticeable tribal difference between the Hones and the Collises. Enid Starkie, in her autobiography *A Lady's Child*, said that tea with the Hones meant cake, tea with the Collises, bread and jam.

Over the generations, the Collises had worked in the professions – doctors, lawyers, Church of Ireland ministers – talented, hard-working, highly respected. Whereas the Hones looked back on generations of painters: the first Nathanial Hone's father was a pin merchant in Arran Quay and must have been sufficiently well off to support an apparently wild son and allow him to go to Paris and study with Gainsborough. There was Horace Hone, the miniaturist, and finally Nathaniel Hone the younger, whose landscapes at the turn of the twentieth century are highly prized today. Of course Evie Hone, the stained-glass artist, carried on the tradition up till the nineteen forties and fifties. Those of the last few centuries were bohemians, travelled, eccentric, and Pat's elder brother, Joe, with his poetic mien and velvet suit, could have lived the life of the dilettante, had he not himself become a distinguished biographer, married a beautiful American woman – the complaining, witty Vera – and settled in a house the far side of Killiney Bay. Fortunately for that generation, their father, although an inveterate gambler on horses and cards, managed to recoup his fortune on the stock exchange, leaving his son enough money to live on without ostensibly having a job. Pat, on the other hand, got a scholarship to Trinity and became a civil engineer, while Kit went off to South Africa to seek his fortune and work in the diamond mines.

After the First World War, the price of diamonds dropped and the miner's wages were cut. They went out on strike and Kit was killed in a riot or drunken brawl.

One letter from him remains. It is dated '1–12–17' and the address is 'Box 225, Benoni, Transvaal'. It begins 'Dear Mary', and in it he apologises for not having written for a long time and wishes her a happy Christmas, hoping that Pat is home. He goes on to say: 'I was down in Durban for a month a little time ago and it was perfect to be out of the mines after pegging away underground every day at the same old thing.' He tells how the doctors say he is suffering from a slight degree of miner's phthisis. Which doesn't mean much after seven years underground, because many men have died after only three years. He puts his survival down to the new precautions which have come into vogue. And then there is the tantalising reference to Mary's letter, which runs: 'And now, Mary, concerning the subject on which you wrote to me. Please leave things as they are. They really and truly can't be bettered; they might be made very much worse. It will be sufficient for me to tell you that if things were not as they are, you can be very certain I should be with Pat in France.' And in the end he begs her to ask Pat to write to him as 'we used to be such friends, with no secrets between us, and he used to have to put up with all my wild eccentricities'.

So what did my mother want him to change? One can only guess at some 'unfortunate relationship,' as she would have called it. Who knows? But to my mind there is an air of tragedy in that letter which underlies its euphemistic tone.

The fact that he died before I was born gave this mysterious uncle a haunting aura of wonderment to my child's mind. At twelve, he had been so beautiful that Orpen saw fit to portray him, a boy with straight hair to his shoulders, in knee breeches and pumps, his hands clasped in the full sleeves of a long coat. His expression, lips pursed, wide-eyed, is one of surprise. As a child, perhaps, he wondered – as he must have when he worked in the mines – at the strangeness of things.

In my family, he was seldom spoken of, yet Pat, my father, told me on his deathbed that the only time he was really happy as a child was when he was playing with his brother Kit.

So there we were in this phoney castle in Killiney, the dog ends of this motley crew, while Joe, Vera and their two children, Nat and Sally, lived across the bay. They lived in mysterious anonymity, as far as we knew. As children, we were not invited, but on one occasion I remember a lunch – an elegant lunch – where there was an extra unused place. Vera explained that she always set this in case the ghost of Granuaile might be hungry. To me, she was an attractive witch.

As the youngest and most inconspicuous of the family, I made little impression on them, but at the age of about two, when sitting in my go-kart outside the avenue, Nat let the brakes off and I went trundling down the hill. I remember the terror, the gathering of momentum; I remember the ride but not the fall. Perhaps there is some significance in this.

My aunt, Olive Symes, this severe Victorian lady, stomped around on crutches. She had only the one leg. A wooden replica reclined in her bedroom cupboard. A great warhorse, my uncle George called her. Early on, our prurience was excited by this phenomenon. The stump of her thigh protruded through her skirts, a rounded end like a club. She liked me because I enjoyed my lessons. She oversaw my scales on the piano, heard my Latin and French, and her approval was warming and unexpected.

Hitherto, my parents and other adults had been wont to look on me as some kind of unfortunate happening. Comments like 'Look what the dog dragged in' were not uncommon. So visits to my aunt's house on the Malahide Road were treats. Cream from the dairy herd of Jersey cows, strawberries from the garden, chocolate cake and a starched maid to wait on us. But like the rest of the Hones, she did not think my mother good enough for my father, her favourite brother, Pat. She adored him, had spoiled him rotten as a child, thought him an Adonis of beauty, so it was essential for my mother to prove herself in other ways, to get away from the snobbish Hones, and her own mother as well – a woman of iron who only had time for her youngest son, Bob. Apart from her father, with whom she had followed the Bray Harriers as a young girl, she was uncomfortable with her family. Her sister, Joyce, an intellectual who later became a Catholic and who was bedridden with TB, and her three brothers, Maurice, Bob and Jack, found her severe and intractable.

She made plans to move inland to a county where she could be a squire's wife, leave printed cards on the doors of the 'gentry', ride out to hounds and paint her watercolours, as she had in India of the paddy fields and plains, and Pat fell in with her wishes.

A small statistic in the scheme of things, I watched the steamer trunks being packed once more, Aiyuni bringing her traps down from the tower, Paloma and I wrapping up our dolls and toy dogs, the live dogs being put on leads and shoved in the back of the Citroën, and the convoy winding its way through Ballybrack, out on the Bray Road by the big tree, through Dublin and on to the Maynooth road, till it came to a stop in the village of Leixlip.

PART TWO

LEIXLIP

Under pressure from my mother, my father had bought a stone-fronted Georgian house, square as a child's drawing, halfway up the Captain's Hill. To the side of this imposing cut-granite building, there was a structure to the right, known as the wing. This was of a different vintage, older, possibly Queen Anne. It was huge and cold as death inside, but we accepted this place unequivocally. It was to be our home for the next fifteen years.

When the Vikings sailed up the Liffey in the eighth century, Thorkils, a reputedly handsome scourge, persuaded his followers to brave the hinterland and push on up the Liffey to its source. After a few days, they may have stopped to admire the silver fish as they jumped and fell and twisted in their efforts to leap the heavy waterfall. Perhaps he saw beyond the possibility of this place being just a spot to rest and feast, and persuaded his men to leave off their carousing and double back to where the waters narrowed and they could ford it to the furthest bank. There may have been a straggle of dwellings already there. In any case, he thereupon named this settlement Lax Hlaup – Salmon Leap.

As the centuries unwound and the Vikings merged with the Celts, or were sent packing, its strategic position, with a constant supply of water, lent itself to industrial expansion. In the fourteenth century, the Normans built a fortification above the original Viking ford. Here, protected on either side by the natural rise of the land, they could command a view of the incoming hordes. Later on, mills were established, the first Guinness brewery was built on the left bank, and merchants built houses, most of which are still standing in the village street. By the beginning of the nineteenth century, the royal canal had been cut, and the railway was built later on. Outlying townlands expanded, and more houses were built. So there we were, planted in the thirties, with all our goods and chattels, our notions and emotions.

When we moved in – dogs, trunks, little girls, Pat and Mary Hone and Aiyuni Cooper – Paloma and I held tight to each other as we tramped the ghost-ridden corridors, poked in and out of the empty rooms, our candles flickering in the draughts. In spite of de Valera's promises, most of the State still stumbled around in the dark. Rural electrification had not yet reached the village.

The village buzzed with the memory of a lorry, carrying the devout from the Eucharistic Congress, that had plunged over the narrow bridge, throwing all its passengers into the Liffey. Ghoulishly, we were sorry to have missed this excitement, and imagined the sodden corpses clinging to their rosary beads as they floated down the river.

Like the rest of Ireland, Leixlip was in decline. The mill on the left bank was closed, and another mill up the River Rye was in ruins. Guinness's brewery had long since moved into James's Street in Dublin. Only Wolfston's rag mill stood majestically, in all its dirt, over the waterfall on the other bank. Leixlip Castle was empty, its sole occupant being an old man in King John's tower at the foot of the avenue. The four shops, Doran's, Dowdall's, Wogan's and Wardell's, sufficed to supply the villagers and outlying farms with provender and stout. The large blanched Georgian house at the entrance to the street stood empty, and only the Miss Mooneys occupied a pretty ivy-covered building across the road. With good humour, they strolled around in their blue tweed coats, dispensing a little charity where they could. Barefoot children with old staring eyes clustered in corners to view the arrival of our cavalcade. Three hovels struggled up the Captain's Hill. A broken necklace of poverty. Up the Georgian Mall, Mr Durkan, of biblical mien, sat in his tennis shoes, reading books. And beside Doran's shop, which sold sweets and cigarettes, and later petrol, stood Joe Breen's forge. Mr Breen, of Goldsmithian proportions, beat on his anvil, awaiting the farm horses as they came down the hill to be shod. *Tick tack, tick tack*, his music filled the street.

All this I absorbed in my sixth year, frightened by the poverty, shy to the point of paralysis, instinctively aware of the ambivalence of our situation, which the rest of the family seemed to ignore. In spite of the Catholic Free State, Protestants still imagined themselves superior, owned most of the richer farms and big houses, and maintained a haughty disregard for the disparagement in which they were held by the growing urban, and largely Catholic, population.

My mother began to cast around for allies. Mrs Dalgetty, an emaciated lady with skin like cork, lived in a mansion called Ryevale up the Maynooth road. Nancy Connell, cousin of my father's and sister of Evie Hone, had a house down the left bank called St Catherine's. She owned the North Kildare Harriers, and my mother prepared herself to follow the hunt every Friday. She purchased a bay mare, and a pony was bought for Paloma. 'She takes to the saddle like a duck to water', my mother, naturally, said. And I followed them to the meets on my fairy cycle (as we called our bicycles), envious of their velvet caps and green jackets.

Paloma and I continued our lessons at the foot of Aiyuni's chair. We translated Caesar, spoke French and slaved over long division.

My mother set about transforming Leixlip House into an elegant dwelling. Brocaded curtains, Chippendale furniture, the paint scrubbed off the mantelpiece to reveal black Kilkenny marble, the double-doored drawing room prettified. She unpacked her ivory elephants, her priceless bowls and jugs, her Spode china (never used), and decorated the shelves with them. Green chintz covers were made for the armchairs and sofas, and we lived in the dining room across the hall.

Apart from high summer, the drawing room remained a freezing, out-of-bounds place. The large chimney billowed smoke. No amount of sugar thrown on the flames cured its habit. We huddled over the stove in the dining room, where we did our lessons and ate our meals on the oval mahogany table.

The basement of the house, a stone-flagged dungeon, became the province of the maids brought in from the neighbouring farms – Annies, Roses, Myras – as they struggled over the recalcitrant iron range. Off this was a scullery with a porcelain sink, with great brass taps like hooded birds, and in the corridor beside the dairy there was a huge meat safe with wire-mesh doors. The dairy was a freezing room with bare concrete walls and a flat counter, on which stood wide bowls. Into these were poured the milk from our two cows. An old-fashioned churn stood against the wall. I loved listening to the slap and suck of the cream as it bounced against the walls of the churn. When the butter was fully formed, the skim milk was drawn off and the butter kneaded into shape with wide, corrugated spatulas. When I was tall enough, I was let make the small round pats. These took care and accuracy.

On the first floor were three rooms, which my mother made an attempt at decorating. Rolls of wallpaper, Georgian green, were pasted to the walls, curtains of flowery chintz were hung on the windows, and in my parents' room, twin beds were plonked, a dressing table with a mirror, and drawers that stuck –

much to my father's chagrin – and a large wall cupboard. Across the landing was my father's study, with table and drawing board, set squares and rulers.

That was it. The third storey comprised the maids' and children's rooms. Damp and drear, with smoking fires and peeling wallpaper. At night, we'd carry up our hot stone jars, our candles, and huddle under the blankets till morning.

In the village, I quickly discovered a lending library. Foyle's Penny Library. Yes, for a penny you could get a book, then return it, and for another penny get another book, and so on. I discovered Zane Grey. I'd devour the novels and at night lie in bed, my book askew, reading by the light of my dripping candle. Later, I found the novels of Sydney Horler and Edgar Wallace, and a wonderful love story called *Captain Desmond VC*. I hoovered the shelves for these exciting yarns. Before this, naturally, I was a consumer of fairy tales, children's books of all kinds, annuals and manuals – whatever I could lay my hands on.

My father had little interest in these goings on. He craved an occupation. He applied to the Shannon Scheme for a job and was turned down. They were only employing Catholics. This was a great disappointment to him. Finally, he hit upon the idea of making kitchen furniture. He rented the empty house at the heel of the village and with local labour started making plain deal tables and chairs and dressers. (The style of which, of course, much much later became trendy.) He believed that traditional furniture could be brought back. So this tall man, in his old tweed jacket, slouch hat and flannel trousers, spent his days happily going from house to factory, his pipe puffing away, vaguely conscious of us children, and happy that his wife was occupied with her social and equine pursuits.

Leixlip House was perched like a vulture between the high wall of the road and an apron of scutchy, infertile fields. A wood of deciduous trees ran like a sickle round the front lawn and dipped into the River Rye at the back of a walled garden. Here apples – Coxes, Worcesters, pearmains, Beauty of Bath and small russet apples, like stones – grew in profusion. Tom Johnston, a handsome six-footer, lantern-jawed, with brown friendly eyes was the 'man about the grounds'. He helped in the garden and the stables, and spent much time sitting on the table in the kitchen gossiping with the maids. He liked to say things like 'Be the hokey', and with his Kildare accent called us 'Great getils'. I spent much time with him, lifting the split wood into the barrow, making hay in the summer, and generally following him like a useless dog.

My mother, however, didn't approve of this laziness, and during the holidays she'd round us up to make us girls work in the garden, picking raspberries, which stood in military rows, and generally digging and weeding – an occupation which bored me stiff. To encourage us, they offered a tennis racket to the first person to pick a hundred pounds of fruit. However, there was not much chance of this: the season usually ended before this task was accomplished.

While Paloma was malleable enough, in my silent grumpy way I'd pick at the tasks, hoping that, by my sheer messiness, I'd be let off. I was up to every dodge to avoid work of this kind, but usually I didn't get away with it. My mother would rant at me to speak, to do, to behave, but in truth we were at odds, and I had no desire to please. On the other hand, I have to admit that I was also frightened. Up until we were about twelve, she was very handy with the cane. But worse still, in a way, were the threats. 'I'll tell your father' or 'I won't tell your father this time'.

Aiyuni studied for her degree in Trinity, lonely, the poor relation paying for her keep; she wept once when she failed an exam. My father railed at her. 'Plenty of people fail exams,' he said and Paloma choked on a fishbone. Sobs gurgled in my throat. 'Stop that noise,' mother said, as she patted Paloma on her back and gave her a drink of water. I imagined the small bones like tines in my sister's throat; my face swelled and burned.

In bed, I asked my sister: 'Can you die from swallowing a bone?' She didn't know. I said: 'When I die, I want to be buried standing up.' 'Why on earth?' she asked. 'So as it will be easier for me to get out. Dying is very dangerous, because they'll bury you alive.' She sat up and gaped at me. 'I'm never going to die,' she said.

Although I paint a picture of parental autonomy, even cruelty, in truth we had acres of time in which to pursue our games. In the dense wood we played for hours, concocting ogres and witches, having picnics with stolen food, racing across the fields, Paloma on her pony, myself on the bike – a rickety old boy's bike which bumped and skidded in the ruts. We taught everything to jump: Neddy, the hard-working donkey, dogs, and even bicycles. Kids from Dublin, whom we got to know later when I was at school, envied this rural freedom – in fact, looked on our lives as idyllic.

The only thing we were afraid of was the storm of bats that filled the air at dusk. When they came into the room, we'd scream and put on bathing caps. My hair, thick and tangled, was a bat-trap. We stood on chairs or hid under the bed. In the wood, bats would knife around like swallows, and we'd run to the old man down the road, who smelled of smoke, and ask him to trap them with his salt stick, as he trapped singing birds to sell for cages. When mother heard of this, she was furious. 'All animals are sacrosanct,' she told him. 'Yes, ma'am,' he said.

Our lessons, still with Aiyuni, put little strain on our intellect. We learnt easily. Looking back on it, she must have been a good teacher. She was mostly patient with me, and my awful habit of standing silently beside people when they chatted, listening in –

or eavesdropping, if you like – irritated the grown-ups beyond belief. My poor mother, particularly, found this silent watching unbearable. And she'd scream hysterically: 'Speak, speak.' This was really the heart of the problem: my silence when I was with her. I was afraid to say anything which might augment her rages.

'Has she spoken yet,' Mrs Dalgetty once asked her in my hearing. Clearly, my obstinate silence was village news! So she screamed at me as usual. 'Say something! Speak, speak!' I scuffed the gravel, and for the first time words came, my chin buried in my jumper. In a whisper I blurted out 'I have nothing to say' and, hiccuping with sobs, I ran into the house, followed by their adult laughter.

But Paloma and Noll made up for my silence. They were great chatterers. It amazed me how words tumbled out of their mouths with seemingly no effort. I don't know what they said that could have been interesting, but to my parents their words were nuggets to be stored and remembered.

AIYUNI LEAVES

At last Aiyuni got her degree. In modern languages. And she must seek a job. What would happen next?

In the crazy way of this dying class, my brother had been sent to a public school in England. Rugby. So it was decided that Paloma must follow suit. She was sent to a genteel school for young ladies in Llandudno in Wales. So when term-time came, they were both dispatched on the mailboat.

What about me? Clearly I had to be sorted out. Finally, my mother heard of a family with a solitary daughter who lived off the Lucan road. A family called Evans. And they had a governess called Creech, short for 'Creature'. Alias Iris Wellwood from Cavan, with gun-metal hair, a short nose and cheeks like plates, on which were dabbed blobs of rouge. I took to her at once. She did not get under my skin, like Aiyuni did, with her coiled red hair and secret sorrow. There was a jolly look on 'Miss Creech' which I considered a good sign.

It was arranged that I take lunch with the family. This lunch – or luncheon – was very different from ours. Salad bowls of fractured glass, carafes for oil and vinegar on a silver tray, tumblers that played the scale. If it hadn't been for Mrs Evans, the meal would have been heaven. Beebe, her daughter, had straight hair, a broad expressionless face, and was as clean as a candle. Compared with me – with my unruly mop of hair, my moonlike visage, the blackheads on my nose, and my brooding eyebrows, which met in the middle – she was the acme of beauty and clean living. Well aware of this, in spite of my being somewhat ahead of her in lessons, she maintained a stiff superior air all through our acquaintance.

Our classroom was as sunny as a greenhouse, and it over-looked an immaculate yard, where the cobbles shone like steel. The whole house was spotless – unlike ours, where dust lay in corners like musty flour. It made me feel even more dirty. Washing in Leixlip House was a perilous occupation. The limey water dribbled into a rusty bath like duck soup, lukewarm and uninviting. Sometimes the whole system broke down and water had to be fetched in buckets from the pump on the hill. So Mrs Evans disapproved. That's what she did best: disapprove. She'd start every sentence with: 'You'd think that . . . '

'You'd think that you'd tidy yourself up.'

'You'd think that you'd brush your hair.'

'You'd think that you'd leave your bicycle round the back.'

'Sorry, Mrs Evans,' I'd grovel, and giggle behind her back.

If it hadn't been for the torturing miles on my fairy cycle, my day would have been easy. Up and down the Spa hill, and then turn off, and another long mile to their house. 'And lay your bike behind the house, don't forget.' In fact, this could have gone on indefinitely if it hadn't been for an 'incident'. I was given to writ-ing rhyming verse in my copybook. I wrote about various sub-jects. Mostly animals. One morning, while I was scribbling away as usual, Miss Creech asked me what I was writing. 'Nothing,' I replied, slapping shut the book. She waltzed over and snatched the book. Up on her podium, she read out the offending lines. It was a poem about gambling. The only line I remember was: 'He had a fortune in his palm.'

'You never wrote this.'

Furious at my literary talents being challenged, I picked up my second copy and hurled it across the room. It hit her slap on the nose.

All hell broke loose.

Mrs Evans was summoned, and she, the woman of Wrath, distinctly said: 'Go, and never come back.'

How could I have been so thoughtless? I'd finally done it. I was damned. Damned forever. My mother had recently been taken to hospital with a suspicious lump on her breast. I could never go home, never, never. My life was in strings.

I took my bicycle from the yard. I had sunk to the bottom of the pit. I had hit my governess and been thrown out of the house.

I took the Celbridge road past the golf club and past Esker, and after a mile or so turned left up a boreen, where two Russians, called Popoff, lived – two tall White Russians with oval heads. I wondered could I kill myself, throw myself over the salmon leap and be battered to death on the boiling rapids below. I carried on into the hinterland, my bike skidding and jumping in the rutted road until a tyre burst and I tried to ride on the rim until I was discouraged by the futility of it. I lay in the grass, the night darkening around me; a cool wind skirted the bushes, animals scuttled about. A man passed on a bicycle, whistling a tune. I pressed into the ditch, afraid of being seen. He passed on, taking his cheer with him. A dog barked in the distance, *Ook, ook*, which ended in a falsetto note like a yawn. There must be a farm near. Afraid of being caught, I heaved myself up and began walking my machine towards home. The weary miles unpeeled, as darkness fell. I crept into the kitchen by the back door and snatched a loaf of bread from the bin and ran up the stairs to my room to hide.

I hid under the bed, stuffing the heel of the loaf into my mouth. Crumbs splattered out; I choked and cowered. But I had to stop chewing to listen, listen for those punishing steps that I knew would come.

When they came, blood sang in my head. I had never been so frightened. I tried to swallow but bread stuck like wool in my mouth. I spat it out and pushed the mess under the bed.

The door opened slowly. Father never hurried except when he was running at cricket. He walked across the room and, with a sniff and a half-smile addressed the window, and the twinkling stars.

'I hear you got the sack.'

That was the nearest I ever got to my father. Those words were to be my talisman in the rough days that followed.

I found a long striped cotton frock of my sister's and, dressed thus, I went to see my mother in hospital. I drove beside my father in the old Citroën with the hood down; the dogs sat in the back, their long legs pegged out like rods. We pulled into the forecourt of the Adelaide Hospital. 'Stay,' I said to the dogs. 'Stay.' Their mournful heads rested on the side of the car in front of the accordion-pleated hood. 'Daragh and Bran,' I said, 'be good.'

My mother lay, looking white and unsettled, in a tilted bed. I stood and stared, silent as the moon.

'Where did you get that dress?'

No answer.

'Speak up.'

'It's Paloma's,' I choked out.

'Go home and take it off.' She held her two hands out to Pat, who bent and kissed her on the forehead.

She came home. Birds swooped on the lawn. A thrush sang. A sweet wind shook the tall chestnut. We helped her from the car – myself and Annie holding an elbow each. They were like shale. She sat on the bench and sniffed the summer. Tom Johnson and another hired hand were scything the meadow field to the right of the lawn. Soon we would all have to work with the two-pronged forks, turning and turning till it was dry enough to pile into cocks. I hovered at her side.

'I didn't mention your behaviour in hospital.'

I ground my teeth. Waited.

'Well, what are you going to say? You've upset your father very much.'

I hung my heavy head and dug the clover with my toe. I turned to go into the house.

'Where are you going?'

'Inside.'

'I can't hear you.'

I continued my journey up the steps and through the front door. I went up to her room and looked out of the window at her. She sat very straight on the bench, her fawn silk dress sagging over her shoulder blades. Her hair had turned grey and wispy; it fell awkwardly in a tangle. The dogs lay at her feet. Pat was taking imaginary golf swings at the clover heads nearby. I rummaged in her chest of drawers till I found a bra with one stuffed cup. I put it round my dress and peered into the mirror. I took a string of pearls and tightened them round my neck. I swung round. Annie was at the door.

'What are ye at, ye brat ye?'

'Oh Annie.' I burst into tears. I sobbed and sobbed.

'Hush. They'll hear ye.'

She held me in her arms. 'I don't understand yez at all.' I tried to undo mother's bra, tried to undo the pearls. My face was smeared, my dress saturated.

'If the mistress catches ye . . . '

'Oh Annie, oh Annie, oh Annie.'

The rain held off, and we turned the hay. The sun set into an orange orb. Before we finished, Mother came out to the field gate to watch. Annie and I had just done the last row. The men plaited the hay ropes and threw them over the cocks. Then we heard her scream. We ran, tripping on the mown stubble. She hung from the gate, one hand on her stomach.

'What is it, ma'am, what is it?' Annie had gone white. We took her gritty elbows and guided her into the house. We put her sitting in the drawing room.

I went out, calling 'Daddy, Daddy.'

Now it was all nervous moving around. Tiptoeing. Afraid of noise. Afraid of her anger when she was upset. It seemed to run out of her like a snake. Paloma, home at last, brought some ease to her. She chatted and gabbled about her exploits at school. She played lacrosse, captained the team. She told mother about the other girls, and mother told her about her schooldays and their feasts in the dorm. They laughed, and the house opened up a little.

She recovered slowly. Summer turned into autumn. Trees shed their leaves. Paloma went back to school. I had nowhere to go. The Evans family were glad to get shut of me.

During that summer, there had been tennis parties. Lady Brooke, a wolflike woman, and her daughter, Alma, equally vulpine, came to tea. I ran hither and thither, carrying trays of tea and cakes and scones. 'Please, can I play?' 'Later.' Always later. Lady Brooke had a laugh like water running into a shore. She and her daughter looked at me as though they had just dug me up.

By autumn, mother had resumed her social calls. Started riding again. Followed the harriers on Fridays. But they assumed I needed to continue my education.

By this time, I had become an average pianist. I would play happily all day. They couldn't drag me away from it – to such an extent that the piano was moved to the wing, out of earshot. There I'd spend happy hours not caring if the keys were damp or the wind howled through the cracks in the large bay-windowed room.

They had tried to teach Paloma but she was tone-deaf. So she gave it up – luckily for the rest of us. The piano was all mine. Only occasionally, father played, and sang songs, which I accompanied. Moore's *Melodies*. Although I could sing in tune, I had a voice like a crow. But he made me sing 'Kathleen Mavourneen'. If anything, I was a sub-sub-alto. As though there was grit in my throat. So the high notes hung in the air like badly oiled hinges.

Advertisements were put in the paper. A Miss Spence was found. She was governess to a girl who lived deep in Meath. She would pick me up every morning on her way from Lucan, where she lived.

Miss Spence was not like Iris Wellwood, did not waltz as she walked. She had her own car. She wore twinsets and had skin like linen. Iris Wellwood had been biding her time till she met 'the man'. Miss Spence was an organised spinster. But she had a Joycean love of opera and classical music. Rare in those days. I had mastered 'The Blue Danube', among other humdrum melodies, but now she took me to the pictures to see Polonaise, and the world opened up to Chopin's *Études* and waltzes. Later came Mozart, and finally Bach. Although I had come across Mozart earlier, quite by chance, when Deirdre Wilkinson was staying and had to practise the piano. 'Oh, do play that again!' I cried, after hearing her piece. To which she snorted: 'It's only Mozart!'

But my stories and poems gave the Meath girl migraine, so very often lessons were conducted with me alone, the smell of toasted muffins wafting up the stairs. I can still smell those cakes and feel the heat from the fire as we sat over it and as I read her my poems and stories. I wrote about animals and wild horses. She was normally even-tempered, but she sometimes got annoyed because she didn't believe I'd written them myself. So to placate her I'd tell her I'd copied them out of a book.

Friends? My frenzied nervous energy was too much for my contemporaries. I always overdid things, which landed us in trouble. My fertile imagination was my undoing. I was forever thinking up pranks. So, locally, apart from the various maids, I had no one to talk to. Beebe was now a wash-out, the Meath girl always sick, Alma Brook a dinosaur of superiority, so my free hours were spent in the fields above Confey with my mongrel dog. And my Woodbines.

Money was hard to find – or steal. I didn't get pocket money but my father's pockets rattled with small change. Two-pence-halfpenny bought four Woodbines in the green open-ended paper packet. Smoking half a Woodbine every day would make the packet last a week. Lying on my back, I watched the sky turn, as I drew in the smoke. The River Rye, which joined the Liffey at the heel of the village, was the apotheosis of my wanderings. Otters slid over the rapids, uttering high cries as the dogs chased them. When you followed the river upstream, you came to the ruined mill – burnt down, it was said, because the villagers couldn't stand the smell of boiling glue, made of animal hooves, which was manufactured there. In the shell of this building, clumps of nettles, cow parsley and dock proliferated. Its worm-eaten beams were perfect for apelike swinging. Beyond the mill and the little bridge, the river tunnelled under the aqueduct of the railway and canal. In winter, icicles hung from the roof, and in summer, water dripped like wine into a glass. Your echo would bang against the dripping stones, ricocheting into the blackness of nowhere. There was a fetid smell from the deep dark water, and I feared to swim there. But further down, I swam from March to October. I had to cross an island plaited with snowberries. Another time, the farmer who owned this land threatened us children with a shotgun. He had a face round and rusty as a hubcap but his imprecations were unsuccessful. We continued to trespass with pumping hearts, our eyes fixed on the distant dwelling. We'd scuttle away like rats if he appeared at his door.

In spite of my mother's being wrapped up in her various pursuits, riding and exchanging visits with the local gentry, there was in her a guarded chasm. I think, perhaps, she was at odds with the world in many ways. Clearly her relationship with her own mother left a lot to be desired. As has been hinted, early on, my grandmother, Edith Collis, born Barton, thought herself to be a cut above the Collises. A branch of the Bartons occupied a large mansion in Wicklow and seemed to live in a much more aristocratic style than the Collises. And the fact that her cousin Robert Barton was one of the signatories of the Treaty added a touch of romance to the family. Yes, my mother was a very frustrated woman – for all I know, sexually, but certainly artistically. Still 'in love' with my father, that handsome man, six foot two in his socks – as we were so often told – she had taken it upon herself to outdo my Aunt Olive's cosseting of Pat, hiding him away from us children as much as she could. He, therefore, to us – or certainly me – had no individuality. He was simply a distant Man of Iron. As I have said, after every misdemeanor there was the same threat: 'I'll tell your father' or 'I won't tell your father this time'. He never punished us physically but, in spite of this, this distant Damocleian sword of what might happen if he found out how bad you were was meant to terrify, and did. On the surface, towards me – except with music – he was vague. But he did really love Paloma, and she loved him. I couldn't understand this love business, and longed to be an orphan. Yes, he was an individual, inventive, with an unfathomed need for doing. When the Germans (there not being enough Irish engineers) finally brought the electric poles to Leixlip, and the village for the first time 'saw the light', my father moved his workshop from the village and built a long corrugated shed the other side of the

Captain's Hill, and here installed bandsaws, fretsaws and lathes, and increased his staff. He began to study the new Swedish designs for plain unpolished furniture. A cabinetmaker, Fergus Peacock, arrived. Although deaf and dumb, he was a talented man, made beautiful inlaid tables, one of which was shown in Canada. We teased him unmercifully, as he talked in loops, and we learnt basic deaf-and-dumb language, as it was called then. We used to giggle outside the lavatory when he was 'at stool', because, unknown to himself, he made animal grunts and loud swishing noises.

As her health improved, my mother decided to expand her social outlets. She began sniffing out avenues of a more cultured nature. Although tone-deaf, like Paloma, she loved Gilbert and Sullivan operas. *The Mikado, The Gondoliers.* When the D'Oyly Carte company came to Dublin, she invited the entire chorus out to tea. The house and grounds were suddenly overrun with tenors and contraltos lolling about, their large limbs like bolsters, spread over the grass. And one, whose name I don't remember, didn't leave. He moved into an upstairs room and sang scales from morning to night. He was as pasty as dough and wore corsets and a toupee. This unpleasant body reeked of stale perfume. He intrigued while he disgusted me. Disgusted me when he ran the back of his hand down my flat chest, intrigued me when he said I was pretty – which made me wonder at his eyesight. I can't imagine what my father, who was genuinely musical, must have thought of this intrusion – this middle-aged, third-rate tenor using up oxygen at breakfast, dinner and tea. My mother, delighted with this ugly intrusion into our lives fussed over him as if he were John McCormack. I do not think that this man did much for her pride, but there were times when her stickle bones relaxed and her eyes brightened.

Edmund Curtis, professor of history in Trinity College Dublin, walked out to Leixlip once a month carrying a box of chocolates, which he presented to my mother with a bow. They would then take tea on the lawn. Frail and anaemic, he had skin the colour of lead. Come half past six, he'd lift his brittle frame and take the bus back to Dublin. I do not know what they talked about or what they had in common, but after his visits, she hummed like a bee.

Another even stranger liaison was that of herself and Pádraig de Brún. He'd stalk up and down, his great head bent as he entered the drawing room. Glorious as a Renaissance statue, he needed whiskey. My father kept whiskey and sherry in the dining-room cupboard, and Monsignor de Brún made short shrift of a bottle during those visits. He sometimes called late at night, roaring drunk, hammering on the front door, waking up the dogs and causing mayhem all round. I was fascinated by this man. Whenever possible, I'd stand beside him and listen. Here was someone who suited my iconoclastic nature. I thrilled from a distance. I don't suppose he ever spoke to me but for a while he filled up the black corners of my mind. I imagined him as an eagle who might one day perch on my windowsill and carry me away.

But in spite of this unexpected alcoholic largesse, neither of my parents drank much. Only once did I see my mother even partially tipsy. She was going to a party and must have had a few sherries. On her way out, she looked into my room and, swaying at the door, gave an arch chuckle. In spite of her beautiful velvet dress, her double string of pearls, her golden pumps, I could not look at her. I didn't know her like this – friendly, not scolding me. I waited stiffly for her to leave.

Yes, the Germans had installed the electricity in the mid-thirties. We listened to their guttural speech as they argued with each other. They wore leggings and brown boots, had cropped hair and khaki-coloured faces. Their shirtsleeves, the same colour as their skin, were rolled up to the elbow. We gazed up at them in wonder. It was all excitement. Soon our house, like the rest of the village, would blaze with light. Candles and guttering oil lamps could be thrown away. When finally the light was switched on, we noticed how dirty our house was. Corners that we barely knew existed were filled with pockets of dust and spiders' webs. An army of cleaners was brought in. Carpets were shaken out, the larder and the pantry were refurbished, classy-looking lampshades were purchased in Dublin. A three-pronged light in the drawing room, resembling a chandelier, was hung with a cream-coloured plate on four chains. The old iron range was thrown out and a shiny Aga cooker was installed. The water system, however, still gurgled and hiccuped, and the bath kept its original map of rusty contusions, to remind us of darker days. But mostly, everything shone. For a while. Gradually the place returned to normal. Only the ground floor maintained a measure of spark.

Yes, the upkeep of the house was uncontrollable. Plaster fell from the upstairs rooms, left craters of rubble. Wallpaper peeled and bubbled, and our bedrooms were as cold and damp as caves. My father had never liked the place. He called it a white elephant.

Reading in bed – a forbidden occupation – became more difficult to disguise. The solitary bulb from the ceiling could be spotted from outside, and my father would roar up: 'Put out the light.' The light switch was at the door, so I rigged up a knotted string, which went across the ceiling, and with which I could extinguish the bulb. But in order to pursue my literary education, I had to raise enough money to buy a torch. This could be awkward, especially in winter, when father didn't often take off his jacket. A pocket torch cost at least a shilling. This was a lot of small change to be creamed off message money or stolen outright. A penny or so was all the wages I got for errands, and with twelve pence in the shilling, the purchase of anything needed a lot of ingenuity.

Meanwhile, I continued to lead my secret life. I still seldom spoke in the presence of my mother, and she began to think me mentally retarded. I was damned by my looks. A very large head – a massive wiry head of hair. A thin angular body. Like a mop held upside down. A slightly protruding jaw under flared nostrils, and eyes too close together. Paloma and Noll had small classical features. There was nothing Neanderthal about them. Thank God no one sent their children to psychologists in those days, because with my inability to speak to my parents, my psychopathic shyness, I could have ended up in an institution. Yes, as I mooched around in this ugly fashion, no one knew what to do with me. The servants called me a changeling. Mother was mortified when friends called. She'd scream at me to shake hands properly. A strong handshake meant good manners. And I had no manners.

Manners were the most important thing in life. Without manners, a person could get nowhere. Clearly I was heading for some unspeakable void from which there seemed no escape. But what could I do? When I was with her, my hand just would not rise from my side. I had to wait for her anger to subside, or for the visitor, who perhaps was as embarrassed as I was, to lead her away from her recalcitrant child, who never did what she was told. I was a wound in her side. Why wasn't I like Paloma or Noll? They shook hands: a strong positive clasping of flesh to flesh. They spoke audibly, glibly. They made eye contact with visitors, with everyone. How did they do it? I tried and tried to copy them, to no avail. There was a stone lodged in my diaphragm. Even entering the village, which I had to do in order to make money, as I said, out of messages, called for a supreme effort of will. I'd stand for ages at the top of the hill telling myself over and over again: 'You can do it.' 'Yes, you can do it.' The shopkeepers called me 'reserved', which was their polite way, I suppose, of saying I was dumb.

Because of this social blockage, this knot of terror, I sought happiness in my endless walks and excursions on my fairy cycle or amongst my copybooks and my scribblings. Paloma would write to me from her boarding school for poems for the school magazine. I gladly occupied myself with this. The poems, of course, were published under her name but I didn't care. It was one of the last few links in a breaking chain.

It seemed a long time now since we'd talked to each other in disguised speech. 'Ermis ermumermy ermangery?' 'Nermo.' 'Sherme ermis ermin Dermumblermin.' 'Germood!' And gone were the days when we learnt all the Jimmy O'Dea records off by heart and would act them out together in the yard. I was always Mrs Mulligan and she was the opposite number. Yes those days had metamorphosed into sophisticated distances. (Incidentally, this speech transformation must have been a Dublin thing, because years later I read in *A Portrait* Joyce's version of this.)

Yes, the goalposts shifted every year. How could I catch up with Paloma's two and a half years, her horsemanship, her social graces, her talent for games? I longed to emulate her. But she was changing subtly. We no longer clung together for warmth like two monkeys. My writings, my Latin and French, were as nothing compared with winning a game of tennis or riding out to the hunt. And my parents put great store by physical prowess, so naturally their adulation for her achievements took precedence over anything I could do. In any case, they knew nothing about me. I'd have died rather than show them my scribblings. As far as my mother was concerned, I was as stupid as a cow. So I applied myself assiduously to sports, practising tennis against the gable wall of the house. I taught myself to ride on the donkey.

My life was a balancing act between these two extremes: aping my sister's achievements and maintaining my inner spirit. But the day eventually came when I felt that the fight was beyond me.

A dog had recently been killed by having been given powdered glass. This gave me an idea. In those days, aspirin came in small glass phials. I took my toy dog, called Dismal Desmond, and sat on the stairs between the first and second floors of the house crunching the glass. Suddenly I was afraid. The blood in my mouth tasted of iron. If I swallowed the shards, I would die. What was this death? Was that not what I had planned? I had never seen a human corpse, although I had often wept over dead puppies or rabbits. There must have been some crazy notion in my head that when they found me, they would feel sorry and I would then get up and say 'I told you so'. That night, I lay in bed stiff and sleepless. Did I really not swallow any glass? I had to be sure. But how could I be sure? Days of this left me schizophrenic. I wanted to tell someone, perhaps Annie. But I would not dare tell her, because in her panic she'd surely run to my mother. I walked the road, I hid in the woods; it was winter, and the thin wind scraped my arms raw. I sat down on a wet cushion of autumn leaves. So, I might not die. 'No, I will not!' I cried. I will not lie like a dead dog with a trail of blood pumping from me like beads or like a rabbit with pink skin showing through my fur.

'She must be dying to go to school,' mother's friend, Connie Hamilton, said one day. 'Is she talking any better?' I felt comfortable with the Hamiltons. Somehow or other, they were not the enemy. Connie's sister, Letitia, was a fine painter, and I felt a thread of sympathy towards the family. Later, someone told me that Connie asked my mother why she treated me like a pariah.

There you go!

However, I was not particularly dying to go to school. Not day school, anyway. Boarding school, now, with all those new clothes, and hockey, lacrosse and tennis, and feasts in the dorm. Everything labelled, everything mine. Not just hand-me-downs – rubber boots and sand shoes, my brother's shorts, cut down to size. But education – if that was what it was about – what of it? Still, with Miss Spence, my lessons put no strain on my intellect. I continued with my Latin, French and sums. It was like taking off and putting on a coat. But school? What really happened in school? Would there be friends? But as I said, my efforts in this department had not borne fruit. I was much more concerned with getting a pony.

Luckily, my mother soon forgot about this, because she had found a new interest. And it was more than an interest. There is no doubt that she had talent and could have been a fair painter had she started earlier. And indeed one or two of her paintings still stand the test of time. So now, under the aegis of the painter Kitty Lloyd, she gave up her watercolours and took up oils, and she and Kitty went on painting excursions to the west of Ireland.

Kitty was a chuckler. She chuckled all the time. She wore an arty fringe and, with her boxy figure, she gave out a continual aura of good humour. Home from these excursions, my mother was gay and lively. They told of funny experiences in the Baby Austin, a wonder car of astonishing age. The house opened up. Instead of my usual sullen silence, Kitty made my tongue work, even in front of my mother. My silly phrases didn't please her, however, in spite of her previous efforts to make me talk, and when Kitty painted me in profile, my mother snatched the painting and turned it to the wall. 'She looks far too grown up,' she said.

Kitty must have spotted something in me, my extreme desire to be adult, free, gone. I was confused. I ran to the kitchen. I stood on a chair and threw all the delft on the floor. I exulted as each plate or glass crashed on to the flags. And then I called the dogs and went up into the fields of Confey. I broke a willow twig and, swishing at the briars, I sauntered up to the railway line. I imagined I could see the Indian women in their saris, proud, with pitchers on their heads. I imagined I could smell the spices in the markets; I walked along the sleepers in the direction of Maynooth. The dogs began to fret, and I called them to follow. We stood aside to let the Galway train go by. Back on the line, I went on and on and on . . .

THE FACTORY

The song of the bandsaw. The decibels rose as Johnny Byrne pushed the heavy oak planks against the wide teeth of the saw. I stood beside him to catch the small wood chips that fell into the sawdust. I knelt in the soft carpet of shavings, collected little squares of wood to make stables for my tin racehorses. He showed me how to make hinges with pieces of leather. The dust made rainbow arcs in the sunlight. I looked at Johnny Byrne some days and said to myself 'I could say "I love you"', and then think about it among the furze bushes on the Moor of Meath. I could say, 'I love you' to nothing, and that meant something. I was growing into twelve and Annie saw the blood on the back of my legs.

She told my mother, who said: 'It has happened.'

I had seen my sister's sanitary towels in a drawer and, not knowing what they were, got the idea of using them to cushion the girth sores on the donkey. I had no idea that they were something to do with a human condition. My sister must have been told not to tell me, but I was always rooting, prying into drawers and cupboards.

What was happening to me? It was hateful, obstructive to my wanderings, my boyish freedom on the wild slopes of Confey. I found a book. The menarche: 'the first flow of blood from an adolescent girl'. Menstruation. It would happen every month.

Blood pouring out of me, down my legs, soiling my clothes, the furniture, the sheets. And to stem the flow I must put these yokes between my legs and rub sores on *my* thighs for a change. And what could I say to my mother? How could I ask her for money to buy them? I practised it. *Please, mummy can I have some money for those things.* Those things.

I couldn't do it. Every month, I tore up rags and stuck them between my thighs, my skin made transparent from painful weals. I would throw the rags into the hen coup and dig them into the muck, where nobody would see them.

I complained to Annie: 'What does it do?'

'It's all to the good,' she said.

'You don't mean that.'

'No. It's a curse. From now on, every month you get the curse. Now you can make babies.'

I was frightened. Babies. Who wants babies?

'I don't want babies,' I said.

She laughed. 'Nobody does.'

Then the daymares began.

As soon as I went to bed, they began. Heavy dough-like creatures tumbled and cavorted on the iron bed-end. I closed my eyes to drive them away, but as soon as I opened them they frothed anew.

Ectoplasmic, they tortured me. Sometimes I had to get up and walk around but as soon as I was back in bed, there they were. When I pushed out with my feet, my limbs became embedded in them. Great cloud-like monsters, driving up my legs.

One day, I got up the courage to ask Paloma if she had daymares. She did not know what I was talking about. I tried to describe them. 'Don't be silly,' she said. I said, 'I thought perhaps everyone got them.'

So I endured them alone. There was no one I could tell about them. No one would believe me anyway.

I don't remember how long this phenomenon continued. But as I got older, I presume they must have stopped. Whatever it was, it was mean and unrelenting.

When Paloma was back for the holidays and in the next bed, I would try to keep her awake by telling her the stories of the books I had read. As I've said before, they were mostly Westerns.

They were wonderful tales, and I would relate the entire plot to her night after night. She often fell asleep, yawning herself into a soundless ball while my voice droned on. I couldn't imagine how she could possibly sleep through such exciting events.

I tried out other writers on her: Sydney Horler, Edgar Wallace, and all those yellow-covered treasures from the lending library in the village. But she still slumbered on.

I found a great black book – *Tales of Mystery and Horror* – and devoured all the stories: 'Green Tea', 'The Monkey's Paw'. I imagined the creature in 'Green Tea' to be perched on a particular wall of an estate halfway between Lucan and Palmerstown. Later, this place became an asylum. Not surprising.

No wonder I had daymares. My head was full of ghosts and ghouls. There was a haunted house near Carton, and here, it was said, the furniture turned upside down every night. And nobody would live in it.

'Will you come with me to the house?' I asked Annie.

'I wouldn't go near it. What's wrong with yez at all?'

Of course, I was really as terrified of tramps as I was of ghosts.

TRAMPS

This is a phenomenon which was very much of those times. These people literally tramped the roads, going the round of Ireland about once a year. So more or less the same time each year, the same ones would appear. They came to the kitchen for tea and meat and chunks of soft white pan. Then they would probably sleep one or two nights in the loft before moving on. There was one I found particularly daunting, although my father always let him in for his tea.

He was a great height, at least six foot six, and he was deaf and dumb. And, like Fergus Peacock, he grunted loudly as he moved. He had his own little home: a large builder's wheelbarrow on which he had fixed a waterproof awning which he slept under, and a built-in extension which he could pull out for a mattress and covers. He used to trundle this up to the Moor of Meath, where he parked for the night.

I don't remember any women tramps, but of course there were plenty of travellers – then called tinkers – who passed by often. They would call you over and tell your fortune and they would do odd jobs and have their tea as well. Later, during the war, the Romanies came, and I used to hide in the ditch to listen to their language. They were beautiful swarthy people, and I used to fantasise that I would one day run away with them. However, they left when the war ended.

Around this time, I got the notion to write a newspaper. So I started making up scurrilous and fictional gossip about the shopkeepers and denizens of the household. How Mrs Doran put peroxide in her hair, how Dowdall's shop was full of horrible boys, how Mrs Wogan had no hair because she had run guns in the Troubles. These stories I typed on my father's ancient machine.

When Patsy Cooper, Aiyuni's sister, came to do the upholstering in the factory and Charles Pilkington brought new ideas for designs, I incorporated them into my columns. Aiyuni, now working in Dublin, still visited often. Before long, it became clear that there was a lover's triangle in progress. Both Patsy, with her wide face and problematic eyesight, who constantly blinked as she worked, as she pulled the hessian over the springs, as she stuffed the horsehair into the ticking, and Aiyuni, with her languid mien and melancholic features, had set their caps at Charles. Yes. They were both in love. Charles was an incipient comedian, had acted in amateur theatricals. He swayed like Noël Coward, wore neat jackets, yellow shirts, and knife-edged trousers of light-brown corduroy. He sported a narrow moustache under a faintly hooked nose and was given to saying things like 'Christ Almighty' and 'Hypothetically speaking'.

I put my money on Patsy: I gave her evens, and Aiyuni three-to-one against. I knew the latter was the more intelligent, for she also read Edgar Wallace, and as far as education went, I never learnt anything after she went away, but she did not seem to inspire masculine love. Of the two, she was the better-looking, with her stunning red hair – but her legs were wrong. She sat with her arms around them, her skirt pulled well down, and with her chin on her knees. It was clear that Patsy was blinking her way into Charles's heart. She was more happy-go-lucky than Aiyuni, and I badgered her for affection, trying to link her wherever she went. She got sick of this, though, me always hanging out of her. I also tried to tease Charles till he became irritated and said 'Christ Almighty'.

I beavered away with my newspaper, inventing scandals and robberies, train crashes and farming tragedies. Children got gobbled up in threshing machines, haggards went on fire. I had a column for advertisements, Kolynos toothpaste, Nuggets boot polish, Bovril and Brands Essence. Slated cottages on one and a half acres of arable land: fifty pounds. I bought and sold cattle and horses. A famous stallion for a hundred guineas, a brood mare for seventy-five. Yearlings for thirty guineas upwards.

Paloma and I saved up cigarette cards, collections of film stars, Grand National winners, dogs. When you got a whole set, there were shops in Dublin that would exchange them for goods. I got a banjo, then an accordion and a suitcase. Paloma, jealous of the ease with which I picked up the notes on these instruments, eventually broke them. So I only had the suitcase in the end, as witness to my assiduity.

I was still traipsing to Meath every day in Miss Spence's Baby Austin, still annoying my fellow student, still learning nothing new.

In the Christmas holidays, Paloma, in her split jacket, jodhpurs and velvet cap and string gloves, cut a dash on her new bay mare, called the Countess. She was a bred mare, and she planned to race her in the point-to-points.

'Lord, give me a pony,' I prayed every night.

After the hunt, she'd have a boiled egg under an egg-cosy, brown bread and butter, and ginger biscuits, which were brought to her on a tray, and she'd boast how she'd been in at the kill.

I went hunting on the donkey and was told to 'Take that fucking thing out of the way.' The only time one heard adults curse decently was at the hunt.

Paloma could be soft-hearted when she pleased. She was, I think, genuinely sorry for my ponyless plight. She shopped around and found an animal fourteen hands high belonging to a farmer in Moyvalley. 'Could Leland have him?' she asked my mother.

'Oh all right', mother said, and off I went with the asked-for price in my pocket: three pounds.

I cycled to Moyvalley to lead the animal home on the bike. A long old hike it was, the pony pulling back and me cajoling it, avoiding traffic and the terrifying long-distance buses, with their billowing tarpaulins, when it shied and skidded, knocking me off my bike time and time again.

I arrived home in the pitch dark, stiff and sore, and threw the animal into the field.

Up at the crack, next morning, I saddled up the animal, which I had christened Nazim, after Napoleon's charger, and commenced the schooling. Obstinate as a mule, it bucked and twisted like a bronco and would do nothing I asked it to. It tripped and slithered over the home-made jumps, and Tom waved brushwood at its rump as the pony reared, entangled in the poles.

'Be the hokey, your ma's gone mad buying that yoke,' he said.

The meet was a few miles from Celbridge. My mother was on a rangy chestnut called Slaney – named after the river near which it was reared. Paloma on the Countess, 'as pretty as a picture', the master of hounds said. My pony annoyed the Whip by his yawing and knocking sideways at the other riders, and when the huntsman blew his horn, the horses scattered into a wide field, over a ditch and away, the dogs in full cry. At the ditch, Nazim stood with his feet planted. I kicked, cursed, slapped. At length, with tears dribbling down my face, I dismounted and jumped the ditch, dragging him over after me. The hunt had disappeared.

Hours later, I walked him home alone, the pony sweating, myself planning murder. I wanted to murder my mother. I wanted that badly.

That evening, when forking hay down from the loft, I attacked her with the pitchfork. She was screaming 'When I was your age, I didn't have a pony!' and I screamed back: 'When I'm your age, I probably won't have one either!' Hatred curled round my spine, and my torso. My legs shook. I could have hit her and hit her and hit her till she lay begging for mercy in the straw, but I threw down the fork and raced across the yard into the kitchen. There I stood at the Aga, trying to steady myself, limp with terror.

'What the hell's got into ye?'

'Nothing. Nothing.'

'I don't know what's wrong with yez at all.'

Around this time, Annie said she was leaving. I was devastated. Although there was still this demarcation line between us and the so-called maids, I truly relied on Annie for friendship, and even affection. 'But why, why?' I asked her. 'Do you not like it here?' She looked sideways at me. She could not trust me. I was still 'one of them'.

After she left, there was a hiatus. Maybe no one wanted to work for us. But there were no factories for women then: the only option open to them was to 'go into service'.

As a temporary measure, a married woman from the village came up by the day. But Mother became paranoid, and imagined that she was stealing her clothes. And sure enough, she was spotted in the village wearing one of mother's cardigans. There was some sort of showdown, but she stayed on to do the cooking and cleaning.

Apart from my long walks and excursions on my bike, I spent hours at the piano. My Aunt Olive paid for the lessons, and every week I attended a woman in Celbridge. Strangely, I don't remember her name, but I didn't like the sort of music she wanted me to play: rollicking marches and things like that. I favoured the more classical music – Mozart in particular – which she thought was boring. Also, apart from the piano, there was the gramophone.

Some years previous to this, the fairy-tale writer Percival Graves – a distant relation of the Hones – had given me a gramophone, complete with needles in the little tin box. 'His Master's Voice', the dog looking into the horn. We had a heterogeneous collection of seventy-eights, with the odd classical ones mixed in with popular songs. One I particularly remember was called 'Poor Papa'. 'Mamma goes here and Mama goes there, but poor papa, he goes no place at all!' But soon the great parental censorship bore down on us, and the record was removed. Also – very important – was the wireless. Radio Luxembourg was on night and day – which provoked a certain amount of heat.

About then, I fell in love with grand opera. Father also enjoyed operatic arias, especially Leoncevallo. He'd sing 'On With the Motley'. But of course also the arias of Verdi, Bizet, Mozart – not to mention the melodies of Moore and Percy French. Many years later, a young woman called Myra arrived one day for work. Although this belongs to a much later period, the importance of this young woman seems part of my whole musical development.

Yes, Myra was different. She sang. She sang grand opera all day long, in particular 'Che Gelida Manina', miming the Italian perfectly. She was beautiful as a film star, with her purple eyes and tar-black hair, and her royal-blue dresses with bloodstains on the back. She slopped around, dropping dishes and burning food, and her singing enchanted me. (She was the heroine in my play *Open-ended Prescription*.)

In those days, grand opera wasn't only for the elite. In the Gaiety Theatre, the gods would fill up, the whole of Dublin there, it seemed. And in the intervals, the audience would break into song, mimicking the tenors and altos, with the easy Italian tunes. I remember a contralto, Patricia Black, who was a perfect Carmen, with her dark hair and Spanish looks. Watching her on stage was like being in some dramatic heaven. Father took me to the Gaiety whenever the Dublin Grand Opera Company came there, and for this I am grateful – not only for having experienced this, but also because it was the one bridge between us that we crossed.

On with the Motley!

One of my parents' favourite words to describe a visitor they didn't like was 'Not very unbending', so I look back at those times around the piano as occasions when my father 'unbent'.

We were not intimate; in fact, he was ruthless if I played a wrong note. And there was no real fun or laughter in this relationship, as one might have hoped. There was always that demarcation line between us and our parents – even with Paloma – over which one did not dare step. I think I was particularly damaged by this, because I was always trying to bridge the gap with humour or jokes, and was not only rebuffed but often severely punished as well. There must have been some rapport between me and my father during these musical times but, possibly because of my mother's determination to share him with no one, he was inhibited from showing any real approval of any of us – except for Paloma's extraordinary athletic achievements. The result was an invisible buffers between us which we could never shift. Nevertheless, years later I wrote a poem in memory of this relationship round the piano, called 'Lines to My Father'. This is the final stanza:

> In Leixlip House, the piano stool
> Was staid, Victorian and worn.
> Outside the squarest Georgian

Of granite carted stone by stone
You, with your wicketkeeper's
broken fingers, played Leoncevallo,
But expertly. I sang,
Who could hardly be called a singer,
'On with the Motley'.

So for any companionship or understanding, as I've said, one relied on the maids. Only for these young women who came and went, those years, until I left home, would have been a friendless void. Even when they couldn't stand up for me when my mother's black moods erupted, I somehow understood. Yet out of their paltry wages – twenty shillings a month – they gave me the odd penny when I did messages for them.

The scarcity of money was a constant bind. I was always thinking up ways of making money. I took unripe fruit to the shops, pretending that my mother had sent me. (That didn't work.) I tried to invent a two-wheeled roller skate. Another time, I bundled up most of my clothes and took them to a rag shop on the quays in Dublin (from which I was abruptly hunted).

Paloma got a monthly allowance of four pounds ten a month, but when it came to *me* needing a few bob, I always seemed to be invisible to my parents! Later on, Woodbines were a necessity. Getting money for them was a constant worry for me. Everyone smoked – my mother, my father and all the maids – and as Paloma grew into adolescence, she smoked Craven 'A' like my Aunt Joyce, who, even though she was dying of TB, chain-smoked with a long black cigarette-holder.

Sex

The sexual life of one's parents remains in the darkness. My parents occupied twin beds – my father, I think, undressing in the dark. Rose, now the mainstay of the house, told me that my mother asked her if she should have another child. That drove horror into my heart. Of course, I knew everything about sex. On paper. But the reality! The idea of the phenomenon filled me with dread. No, no! Anything but that.

My mother, to me, seemed far too inhibited for anything remotely connected with sex. You'd as much embrace a blackthorn hedge as give her a hug! But I suppose, looking back on it, it was not her fault that she gave this impression. It was her mother, and her mother's mother's mother, deep into the tunnels of time. Rigid Protestant mores, harking back to Victorian hypocrisy. Children overlapped each other like puppies in a box: did any of these women ever enjoy their sex life? Wives died of overproduction and were replaced.

But in my parents' generation – that is, in the upper and middle classes – the numbers in families had dwindled. There must have been some sort of workaday contraception. Or simply abstinence?

Anyway, my mother had clearly planned two children in the beginning, and having a boy and a girl seemed perfect. So this left me wondering why she would contemplate having another child. I was the one mistake, she told me. This was bad luck. Yet how did it happen? Did my father, in a moment of frustration, leap into her bed?

She had once been a golden-haired girl, claimed to have been a suffragette, said she would have thrown herself under the king's horse if she'd been there. I try and try to fathom what went wrong. I never knew her. I knew of her. I knew her as a woman coiled up with anger. And she was tired. Always tired. Sometimes she was so tired that speech came out of the side of her mouth.

In rain or shine, if I escaped without being seen, I left the house early, not to return before nightfall. I didn't care if my wet clothes clung to me like a second skin. I didn't care if I was hungry. I just kept meandering, sometimes on my bike, sometimes on foot. When the water in my clothes froze, I broke the ice with my hands. I was contented. I sang my songs and talked to my dogs, a selection of mongrels: Kerry blues, greyhounds and collies, all mixed up. And I smoked.

When I got the pony, of course, awful as it was, I was deliriously happy. I'd ride to the Moor of Meath, a place I loved, and when the days lengthened, I'd dismount and lie among the furze bushes, the blue smoke curling in the February air, the pony grazing beside me.

When we visited my Aunt Olive Symes on the Malahide road, my mother was cautious. My mother did not trust her sister-in-law. So usually we went alone. In the holidays, Paloma and I would take the Malahide bus on Eden Quay and walk up the avenue to Lime Hill, a square yellow mansion among beech and chestnut trees. And as I said earlier, there we were, spoiled and cosseted. Her ancient maid, Mary, slow as a steamroller, welcomed us open-armed. We were never too young to play tennis, so I put on my coat of good behaviour and gloried in it all. And there were friends to meet – Rachel Blair White, and Margaret

Hutchinson in St Douglas, where we sometimes had tea and played pass the parcel, ludo and halma, or twenty-five.

As I have said, the extraordinary thing was that my Aunt Olive really liked me. I used to tell Paloma that if she died, I'd die too. Paloma, as usual, thought me off my head.

But on many occasions, my crazy energy got the better of me. The house in which Nathaniel Hone the younger had lived was on the other side of the road. This imposing mansion, then empty, the large rooms, with their flapping wallpaper and broken windows, would be an ideal place to bring my followers. The very fact that it was out of bounds was enough to spur me into action. Creeping through the shrubbery one day, I led three or four children into the house, and there we played, our voices echoing in the ghostly rooms, our footsteps clattering on the bare boards, with a feeling of expanded freedom. Of course I was punished. I didn't care. I was unimpressed that this place had once been inhabited by a famous painter; I had simply broken the rules, and been happy.

Looking back on that escapade, I often think that had I been older and with a little more sense, I might have found a torn morsel of a canvas or a discarded drawing, because I remember that the floor was littered with scraps of paper. But . . . Well . . . but!

THE FACTORY

The song of the saw was silent. Johnny Byrne had lost a child. He wouldn't come to work. The scourge of TB. One by one, children sickened and died. And his youngest son succumbed. Father raged: 'It's only a child.' When he did come back to work, he became careless. He'd cast the planks from the bandsaw with hatred. When cutting a plank one day, the teeth caught his thumb, and it went flying into the sawdust.

'Throw the master switch, for the love of God!' The men shouted.

This episode, and my father's reaction, his saying 'It's only a child,' lay for years like dough in my stomach, until, in *That London Winter*, I wrote it out.

I was there when it happened. I had seen the thumb like a bloody sausage spinning in the air. I had heard the slow deceleration of the saws, seen the paralysis on the men's faces as they moved in slow motion to the aid of their mate.

Yes I was inadequate, as I always was when it came to a crisis. I ran out of the factory, up the hill to the house. I sat down at the piano, hammered out Liszt's piano concerto, thumping the loud pedal, banging the keys. I was frightened out of my wits.

My mother tried to bring some help to the wretched Byrne home. It was one of the meagre houses, damp as a cave, next door to the dressmaker from whom I'd learnt the notes of the piano. She'd send me down with some offering – a few cakes for the children, an old coat for Mrs Byrne. I'd force myself into their house, stand awkwardly at the door, smelling the sickly aroma of unwashed clothes, grease and all the attributes of poverty, a little middle-class waif with no social graces, no ability to speak in normal tones, just a swallow of words before making off as quickly as possible.

'God has left us,' Mrs Byrne said, her hair trailing across her eyes, her torn dress half covered by an apron.

I knew nothing of this. To me, the Catholic God was kinder than the Protestant one.

Every Sunday, we streeled to the pretty church in the middle of the village and suffered an interminable sermon from a clergyman who knew all your sins. It was boring listening to his long, affected vowels, and when at last he said 'And naow to Gawd the Father, Gawd the Holy Ghost', his doughy mouth slapping the words, we couldn't get out fast enough.

I came to envy the Catholics who went to Confession, although the notion of confessing my sins to an old man was terrifying. Yet they got rid of their sins that way, whereas we carried them round on our backs, bewildered and guilty. God sees everything. Sees the half-crown you stole from your father and, worse still, sees into your head. Knows you have murder in your heart, want your parents to die. Death seemed the only solution – the only way in which one could free oneself of this monstrous burden. God worked through one's parents, and I foolishly believed that, if this halfway house was eradicated, my guilt would vanish.

My poor mother, with her snobbishness, her courting of the gentry, Colonel this and Lady that. The Honourable Mrs

So-and-so. The hunting circle, the Anglo-Irish meadows. In one of his letters, my father wrote from the trenches that clinging to the Empire was foolish.

Still you must remember dearie, that the tale of Ireland bears as acute a tragedy as any here and if you are faithful and consistent to your ideas as regards the relations between Ireland and England there is nothing wrong in seeing Ireland as your goal. That I mean is the legitimate reasoning of the Sinn Fein — just the ordinary course of thinking. That is why I cannot defend your attitude and Olive's re. the Rebellion. To say, So many lives thrown away for a foolish cause or an imaginary cause etc, applies with equal force to any war and very strongly to the European War, as perhaps Olive would indeed admit but would you? . . . There are more interesting things going on in Dublin than in this miserable front.

So what had happened to my mother's apparently revolutionary teenage notions? Or were they fake? That my father was hinting this with his 'but would you?' I find interesting.

I can't help wondering also how he'd have been had he not joined up, and not been part of that disastrous conflagration, and how this must have made him see many things in a very different light from how he would have been brought up to see them.

Sometimes there were heart-rending asides in his letters:

When I left Canada I didn't mind leaving my winter things there. To tell the truth I didn't really think there was any prospect of ever wanting them again as I didn't think coming back from the war was in the region of likelihood.

These sorts of comments were rare. He always tried to maintain an optimistic outlook, telling of funny escapades or games of cricket or football or cards.

As I said earlier, Pat Hone left the Canadian Pacific Railway to 'join up', as it was called, as an ordinary soldier, like many another person who believed in the fight for small nations, which turned out to be the bloodiest massacre the world has ever known. Orchestrated from Whitehall, millions died, as is now known, unnecessarily. So Pat, a simple man with a number, offered himself as fodder to this killing machine. He would have remained an ordinary soldier had my mother not kept bludgeoning him to get a commission.

In one of his letters, he argued about the futility of trying to get a commission but she, and possibly her own father and his sister Olive, put pressure on him. And since he was after all a civil engineer, he eventually became a captain. Although when he came to live in Leixlip, because we lived on the Captain's Hill, people were often confused, thinking that the hill was named after him.

He hated this, often pointing out that he had never belonged to the British army and that his commission was only for the duration of the war.

But here again, my mother would sometimes introduce him as: 'My husband, Captain Hone.'

KILLINEY

THE COLLIS FAMILY

Of course, we still visited Killiney regularly. These visits were often painful for my mother. On Christmas Day, especially, rows would erupt, usually between her and her younger brother Bob, one of the twins. And when I read *A Portrait of the Artist* years later – the first 'real' book I read – having discovered that James Joyce was not a woman (!), he recorded the exact phrase that haunted my memory of those embarrassing contretemps: 'On this day of all days.'

But for us children, these Christmas dinners were fun. We were allowed a glass of wine each, and afterwards my Uncle Bob, relaxed and merry, would direct charades. Clothes were brought down from the attic and all sorts of madness would ensue.

When I was about six, I'd ride in the dickie (the folding back seat) of my grandfather's Morris Cowley with Dickie Roper, a neighbour's son. We'd cuddle together, swearing eternal love. Strangely, the grandparents didn't seem to think this an immoral carry-on, and with a certain benignity they encouraged our childish courtship, or at least smiled on it. I think the courtship fizzled out rapidly because, years later, I met him again. He had not grown much, and was a poor weed, I thought. He had a job as a floor-walker in Woolworth's.

But to go back to the Collises. When I was nine, my Uncle Bob got married. The wedding was to be in Cornwall, where his wife-to-be, Phyllis, lived.

She came from what seemed to be a jaunty household. Her father, a lean man, ran around in sand shoes. This must have suited my uncle, Bob Collis, with his broad outlook and speedy friendly manner.

Paloma and I were to be bridesmaids. The family trundled across to England and, although I don't remember the wedding ceremony, I needless to say disgraced myself by falling down a cliff which sloped steeply to the sea. On this breathtaking descent, I tried to clutch at stones or heather, and at one point a stinking fish corpse, as I sped into the deep dark waters below. I should have drowned. But by dint of swimming under water, I was able to grab at an outcrop of rock and lever myself up. Could I never be sensible, like the rest of them?

My Aunt Joyce, whom I have already mentioned, an intellectual, dying of TB, spent most of her time in bed. She eschewed the Protestant faith by becoming a Catholic, and wrote a book about her conversion, *The Sparrow Hath Found Herself a House*.

Then there was Maurice, the eldest son, also an intellectual, with a love of 'modern art', as it was then called. This confused my grandmother. 'Nothing looks like anything,' she said, although she slyly admired her eldest son, who had been in Burma in the capacity of District Attorney and, because of his liberal views, was practically ostracised by the right-wing upholders of the empire. His book *Trials in Burma* reached almost cult proportions amongst the new liberal-thinking literati between the wars.

So that left Jack, Bob's twin. Jack, like myself, was ignored by his mother. She had no time for him. Bob, the apple of her eye, an international rugby player (three or four caps for Ireland) and already ensconced in the Rotunda as a forward-looking paediatrician, held all her maternal affection. Jack, therefore, having escaped to England, was not seen much of in those days. Years later, when we finally became good friends, he said simply: 'I never had a mother.' And this was also long after he, too, had become an interesting writer, an ecologist long before his time, and no mean stylist.

All those literary forebears! No wonder I inherited the writing bug. And bug it certainly was. Although some years there were gaps when I didn't put pen to paper, I always knew that the bug was there. In a television interview recently, I was asked: 'When did you decide to become a writer?' 'How do you mean "decide"?' I answered.

But as for those Killiney years, as children, we thought more about the tea and scones we would get there, and ignored the interplay of adult emotions. They were not cosy people, my grandparents. No sweet old lady knitting by the fire, no genial old gent bouncing you on his knee. So we put up with them, without complaint. That was the way of things, and we accepted it.

In my novel *The House*, I have fictionalised this family, writing from the point of view of Maurice, and changing the period to suit the story. I have always been pleased with this novel, because I think I have captured the characters of the five siblings and their parents with a slant of accuracy in my endeavour to portray the Protestant professional classes in all their ambiguous relationships with the new Catholic state, while emphasizing the chill of the Church of Ireland ethic.

School

My brother went to Trinity, I went to Alexandra School. I was thirteen and heading into frumpy adolescence.

At seven forty-five, I levered myself out of bed to make breakfast in the kitchen, to put the frying pan on the stove, the fat rashers and sausages. He'd say, 'I can't eat this greasy muck', and before long we'd be piled into the Baby Austin and he'd drop me at Nassau Street, throwing the satchel out after me.

I wore my cheap Pims blazer – my mother thinking it a waste of money to be buying the regulation one from Brown Thomas – and she sewed the letters 'ASD' on the pocket, my brown gym tunic, my long brown lisle stockings, held up with garters, and my strapped brown shoes. All in all, a sorry sight.

At other times, I took the 66 bus at eight fifteen, listening for it as it stopped and started all the way up the village street.

Mr Lane, who was now my father's secretary and accountant, doled out fourpence every day for my tram fare. If I ran all the way up Westmoreland Street, round by Trinity, up Kildare Street and round Stephens Green East, I'd save the money for a Mars Bar.

My tunic hung like two boards in front and behind, solidified with grease, and it clanged against my knees as I tried to beat the clock. Late for prayers, I'd sneak in, hoping not to be seen. I always was. I didn't care.

In fact, for the first time in my life I didn't care about anything. Simply getting to school, sitting at my desk, going from classroom to classroom. Racing through town at four to catch the four thirty bus from Aston Quay.

There was no time for anything else. I'd stuff bread and golden syrup into my mouth and sit on the Aga doing my homework. Bed. Reading. Listening to the church clock as it chimed its chimes, until eventually I fell asleep and the day began again.

School was neither dull nor interesting, so in order to make it interesting I developed a talent for playing the fool. And organised crime. Graffiti in the long damp piss-house was practised assiduously by myself and the only Catholic girl, Joyce O'Reilly. We wrote 'Fuck' and 'Shit' on the walls, we mitched in the afternoons, we spent hours in Woolworth's, stealing rings and brooches, racing down Grafton Street, pissing ourselves with laughter.

Like a train running into buffers, my interest in learning came to a stop. What I knew already – Latin and French – had me way ahead of my peers, but my abysmal ignorance of history, geography, religious education (most hated of subjects) and even English literature caused me to stare moronically out of the window for hours at a time. My maths was also minimal, and in spite of the beauty of the maths teacher, Miss Dove, I was lost in a tangle of geometry and square roots.

Yes, Miss Dove was beautiful. And filthy. She reminded me of my Myra. All the years I was in school, she wore the same orange dress, with gaping holes under the armpits. Her short black hair swung round her perfect features. Around her warm thighs, a soiled petticoat hung in tatters. And she was a genius, we were told. But she couldn't teach for toffee. In a sing-song voice, she'd talk from the blackboard, scratching up theorems and unsolvable problems about trains going at different speeds. Eventually, to my mortification, I was moved down a class – to the B section, where a lady as old as a mountain, with a blonde moustache, elucidated quadratic equations. To my amazement, I found myself at the top of the class. The others must all have been dunces! The result of this was that they copied my homework as soon as I arrived. This didn't mean, however, that I became a mathematical genius. Far from it. But I was great at the algebra! And also at tying my India rubber on the end of the blind cord and slinging it at the blackboard, whereupon Mrs Burns would turn slowly round and gaze sternly at twenty innocent faces hiding their hysterical giggles behind dirty handkerchiefs.

But she was far too old to punish us. A pushover.

Miss Ardagh, the French teacher, became the object of my 'pash'. Everyone was expected to have a pash on one of the teachers. She always wore a green overall covered in white chalkmarks. A rotund woman in her mid-forties, she favoured short, straight, mouse-coloured hair. Under the overall, one occasionally glimpsed a fawn woollen dress, which hung below her knees over her lisle stockings. She had brown strapped shoes, and these squeaked like puppies when she walked. A useful trait, as it warned us to be quiet when she approached.

But the demon was Miss White. She was a woman who seemed as though she was the same age all her life. About four foot nothing, with breasts that stuck out like platforms, she had the knack of inspiring terror in the hearts of the staunchest. She taught Latin, and by the fluke of my peculiar education up till then, I had the edge on all the others in the class.

In between classes, I attended Mr Barry for piano lessons. This was a risky business.

When I played well, he put his arm round me, murmuring 'Good, good'. But when I bungled anything, he became a ball of rage, hammering my fingers with his ruler. Because I loved my lessons so much, I'd leave the room in floods of tears. I'd have to stand outside my next class until the gulping sound subsided.

Mr Barry was the organist at St Patrick's Cathedral. He must have been the oldest man I'd ever seen. A tiny creature, with a long wrinkled face. And I worked so hard to please him as he sat beside me, his back bent like a sickle, the long brown mac which he constantly wore, a garment built up with grease, draped round his knees.

Miss Smith, the Irish teacher, like a slapstick comedian as she jerked and joked, had no time for me, who was five years behind the others. In desperation, I learnt off the poems by heart, loving the old calligraphy, and when exams came I'd fit them into the paper. Then Miss Haithornthwaite, the singing mistress. 'Nymphs and Shepherds', '*An Maidrín Ruagh*'. Because of my crow-like voice, I usually accompanied the others on the piano. But believe it or not, our choir was once recorded in the old Henry Street building of Radio Éireann, and the current maid said that she could distinguish my voice. (I'm not surprised!) Like the arts class, these hours were a relief from the endless tedium of lessons. And of course, the games mistress. By now I was an expert hockey player, running the team with Joyce O'Reilly, she right wing, I left. We had much in common. She wrote plays, I wrote poems, and every year, with a sigh from the assembled company, I was given the poetry prize. A book I won, which I treasured for years, was an anthology edited by Yeats – a book that should be republished.

Joyce was also into sex, a subject that lurked like a monster somewhere in my subconscious. Everything below the belt being taboo in our household, my hands never strayed amongst those nether limbs, apart from one isolated experience – more about which later on. But Joyce, a strapping working-class girl, seemed to have none of my inhibitions. She set me up on a date with her brother.

A creased brown photograph portrayed a nonchalant figure in a cap. I suppose he must have been about eighteen. The figure was leaning against a lamp-post as if he had all the time in the world to seduce innocent girls. I did not think him good-looking. However, he was male, and therefore I agreed to meet him at the Metropole one Saturday afternoon.

Outside the Metropople, I waited, having told my parents I was playing a match against the Ursuline Convent. (Where we loved playing, incidentally, because of the fabulous teas we got. And how us snobby Alexandrites used to laugh at their Dublin accents. 'Follee it up!' they always said. 'Follee it up!')

Anyway, with this lie well established, I waited, waited, waited. People went in and out, couples met, hugged each other and disappeared into the mysterious wonderland of the cinema.

I took the bus home.

'You're back early.'

'The match was cancelled.'

'Why did your brother not turn up?'

'Did he not?'

Yes, the hormones were at me. I had lost the capacity to learn. I grew fatter and uglier by the minute. My head was enormous. Hydrocephalic. My jaw, Neanderthal. My brother would rather be dead than be seen with me, and I must say I couldn't blame him. (His favourite way of addressing me was with a list of epithets, among them Face-ache, Vim Tin and Toast Rack.)

Years passed. One by one I did well in French, Latin and English, abysmally in other subjects. I plastered my face with lipstick after school and still stole jewellery from Woolworth's to give to Paloma, in a belated attempt to keep in her good books.

In the mornings, when I was detailed to go into the parents' room to say 'I'm off', I stole the change from the chest of drawers, on which my father had emptied out his pockets. And stuffed myself with Fry's chocolate bars, and penny chews.

There was less communication than ever between me and my mother. She knew nothing about my school, except for one occasion when, in a state of mortification, I was obliged to see her in the audience when I was playing the king in *A Midsummer Night's Dream*. Her presence embarrassed me so much, as she sat awkwardly on the side of her chair, that I forgot my lines and ruined the whole play.

The only saving grace in my final year at school – when I should have then gone on to Alexandra College and thence to university – was getting a scholarship to further my French studies for a month at Neuchâtel in Switzerland. This I would take up after the summer holidays, and then return to Alexandra College to continue my lessons up to entrance exam to Trinity. But my Aunt Olive – misguidedly, I must say, in retrospect – jumped on this and said it was a wonderful opportunity, and she'd pay for me to stay three terms in the pensionat. Naturally, bored stiff as I was with my school curriculum, I was over the moon, thrilled with the notion of going abroad.

Possibly the worst thing about Alexandra School was the presence of the 'Clergy Daughters'. These were the poor Prods who boarded, who had come from poverty-stricken livings in the country and were allowed to pay half their fees. They were an obnoxious crew, goody-goodies who told on you if they caught you at some prank or misdemeanour. They swashbuckled around in their hideous gym tunics, keeping an eye out. You never knew when you'd run into one – to your detriment.

To annoy them, Joyce and I spent a lot of time in the corridor on each other's shoulders, looking out of the high windows and hoping to catch the eye of a UCD student, or envying the girls from the Sacred Heart in Leeson Street. Envying their pretty purple dresses and white lace collars, which, compared with our dreary brown uniforms, seemed the height of elegance. We were always told not to watch them; years later, I heard from one of them that they got the same advice from their teachers about watching *us*.

As I said, I had become an inveterate liar. Two-faced, sucking up to the teachers and taking the piss behind their backs. For this reason, Miss White called me down one fine morning and, instead of saying, which she usually did, 'I'm very disappointed in your marks', she said she had decided to make me a prefect. This was my chance. I'd 'take' the corridor at lunchtime, lurking in corners, yelling at the girls to walk in single file, to stop talking, while at the same time mimicking a teacher's voice in my cut-glass accent so perfectly that everyone was taken in. Of course, this was a risk I milked to its end. Eventually my badge was removed. In fact, I was nearly sacked. Another Evans debacle.

PALOMA

Paloma was now considered a beauty. She had inherited the fine bones of the Hones and Coopers, whereas I was stuck with coarse looks: my contemporaries considered my face to be like the back of a bus. But she had the same sort of features as Lauren Bacall, especially as she grew older: that slightly dissipated look, the hair falling heavily to one side and curling under her chin. She was oozing with charisma and what we used to call 'S.A.' or 'it'! Surrounded by admirers, she occasionally deigned to tag me along. Her friends were all young men who rocked on their heels in admiration. When *I* was addressed by one of them, the paralysis of shyness turned my tongue to putty.

'This is Childe,' she'd say enthusiastically. ('Childe' was the secret nickname we used for each other.) 'She speaks French.' Fat lot of good that did. They were mostly horsey people, rough and attractive, who smoked holding the cigarette backwards with thumb and forefinger, and taking great puffs into their lungs. She was now a highly skilled horsewoman of international class and was riding in the RDS. We'd sit together in the pocket of the jumping enclosure laughing at dirty jokes till it was her turn to mount and enter the ring. She had one great horse, an eye-catching roan, Oloroso, an ex-steeple chaser which she had bought for ten pounds and on which she is still remembered as having collected many prizes.

I did all the dirty work, grooming, mucking out, glad to tag along in this esoteric milieu, hoping that one day, I, too, might be out there in the dizzy heights, clearing fences to thunderous applause.

In the evenings, we'd trudge through the main hall. I was still young enough to enjoy collecting samples there: Nugget Boot polish, tiny jars of Lamb's jams, squares of Bournville chocolate. And, weighted down with tack, we'd repair to the Horseshoe Bar across the road. Here we'd be ensconced, Paloma's every word a jewel to be grappled for, as the pub filled up with members of the Irish army team – Captain this and Major that – while, dumb as a board, I stood beside them.

She drank seriously now and, for a year or so, I was afraid to follow suit. Until one day, one glorious day, I had my first taste of alcohol – the all-healer, the lady of forgetfulness. It was a miracle. Suddenly my tongue loosened. Speech that had been dammed up flowed unstinted. I was funny – I found I could make people laugh as I had at school with the other girls. Unfortunately, I had to rely on Paloma for her largesse. And she didn't always shell out. A pint of stout was eleven pence, cigarettes ten for sixpence. My continuing poverty was a scourge.

After these excursions, I was usually sent home while she went I knew not where. I guessed she wanted to be alone with one of the men. That she would have 'sex' with one of them was obvious, but I was never allowed to ask. My single experience in this department I kept to myself.

No one knew that at the age of twelve, I had been kissed by a young man at the foot of the Captain's Hill. It was my brother's eighteenth birthday, and my father was holding a dance for his son. The factory was cleared of machinery and a wooden floor laid over the stone one. Yes, he was giving a party for his eldest child.

Undergraduates from Trinity were invited. Paloma was bought a silky gown of green satin and I got a short white dress with puffed sleeves.

I poured olive oil on my thick hair and tried to iron it flat. I spent hours looking into the wing mirror, hoping that if I turned my head sideways, people would only see my profile. A fine evening in May, the company strolled across the Captain's Hill in all their finery, while the villagers turned out to see how the other half lived.

My heart rocked and I imagine, as in all subsequent dances, I was relegated to wallflower status. So how was it that during the night I found myself in a Baby Austin beside a Jewish eighteen-year-old who had his hand up my knickers? I do not know. I do not remember his name, but I remember him.

I was at the bottom of the hill in a car with a man who could have been twenty and I was being kissed.

'Don't be afraid. I'll give you a thrill.'

'No, no.' I grabbed his hand away and he kissed me again.

The band blasted away in the factory. There was music and dresses and black suits with bow ties, and I was in a car with a Jewish boy who had kissed me. In the passenger seat of a car, and he had opened his mouth and licked the inside of my mouth and saliva had dribbled from our lips.

Nothing lasts. Especially something as earth-shattering as the experience of your first kiss. Hands began to scrabble at the window, voices were raised. 'She's down there . . . I saw her half an hour ago . . . Was no one keeping an eye on her?'

Yes, it was an experience of a kind. The fact that I had brushed his hand away, terror of his touching my nether regions uppermost in my mind, meant that the kiss was everything. The Kiss. The first Kiss. Can one ever forget it?

What was his name? How did I know he was Jewish? Was he Aaron, or Jacob, or David? Was I dragged, escorted gently out of his car? Was I told I shouldn't be there, asked how I had got there, and told it must be time for my bed and I might lose something.

I had not lost anything but didn't say, because I was meek as a fawn and didn't want trouble, and everyone was enjoying themselves so much that *they* didn't want trouble either, and the whole thing blew over rapidly and I never saw him again.

Yes, Paloma, with her superior knowledge of the facts of life, was quite unaware that her baby sister had also had an 'experience'. I would watch her run her gloved hand along the railings in the pocket of the enclosure. 'How are the gee-gees?' The burning question while everyone prayed for spavined hocks and sprained fetlocks. The beautiful Irish army chestnut Limerick Lace was ready to go. 'I hear Kellets got a new horse.' 'Since when?' One of her admirers, a man from Meath with stone-blue eyes, said: 'Oh ho, the sister. Sex and the gees can't be bet.' I bravely told them about a man who gave his horse a bottle of stout every day and it thrived. An officer said 'Really?' They talked about horses coming in poor from bad clover land in Westmeath. 'Sure it's all fucking bog there,' the Meath man said. All this I recorded in the beginning of my first novel, *Girl on a Bicycle*.

And so to the songs and stories in the Horseshoe Bar:

> *South of the border, down Mexico way.*
> *That's where I fell in love, where stars above came out to play.*
> *The mission bells told me that I mustn't stray.*
> *South of the border, down Mexico way.*
> *Aye aye aye, Aye aye ayyye.*

'Do you remember the brother's dance,' I ventured one day to Paloma.

'What about it?'

Paloma was such a phenomenal horsewoman that Joe Hume Dudgeon paid for her to go to England and take the exam which would make her Master of the Horse. This entailed written as well as practical work. She passed it easily.

Later, as will be seen, when she finally married John Price her career went downhill. Although she later instituted women riding under the rules in flat races in Zimbabwe, then Southern Rhodesia.

Back to the shows and Ballsbridge hideouts. Playing poker on upturned crates in the stables, me the willing dogsbody, glad to tag along.

Apart from all this, she could charm the birds off the trees. At one time, the whole of Dublin seemed to be in love with her, and yet she seemed in the end to have made a hames out of it. Her premature death in her fifties ended a life fraught with sexual upheaval, without having really achieved any of her potential.

CRICKET

In spite of this seemingly sophisticated lifestyle, I was still inde-cisive, racked with daymares and nightmares, bad memories haunting me.

The child is eight. She sits on a fence in the Phoenix Park. Her father is playing cricket. He is playing for Phoenix against Leinster Cricket Club. He is the captain. Phoenix are in. Ingram is at one end, Pat at the other.

Everyone watches. Mummy, Aunt Olive, Uncle George, Grandpa . . .

Ingram makes forty-five not out and they draw stumps for tea. There will be tea in the clubhouse. Flat cake called Foundation Cake, thinly sliced white bread and butter, and rasp-berry jam.

But the child can't move from her perch on the railings. If she does, she will wet her knickers. She wriggles from side to side, beads of sweat gather under her armpits and slide down her dress. She sees, or half-sees, the players entering the pavilion. She sees, or half-sees, her father shedding his gloves, laying down his bat. She thinks he scored a boundary. But for the last half an hour, she has only been able to concentrate on one thing. Not letting go of her pee.

Then it comes. It runs. It cascades, floods the back of her dress, her socks, her sand shoes. It trickles on to the grass. It steams. Her dress is warm and stained, her socks discoloured. She is paralysed with shame.

'Tea!'

She stays on the railings. She has no idea what to do.

Yes, my father was a brilliant cricketer. It was his one great love. *Wisden* was his bible. As a child, he'd been photographed beside W. G. Grace in Kildare Street. When he retired, he wrote a book called *Cricket in Ireland*. He claimed that all his family played first-class cricket and that they once fielded eleven Hones in the same team. But he was supreme. He had played cricket in England for the London Irish. He captained the Gentlemen of Ireland for many years, and whenever he could he went to Lords or the Oval in London. As a little girl, I pictured Lourdes as a well-tended field, with laconic figures in white throwing red leather balls at each other, and marvelled at the reason why Catholics wanted to watch cricket!

Yes, for a while the game seemed to dominate our childhood. There was a week when the house was full of Indians. Plump dark men trundled up and down the stairs, their Anglo-Indian voices singsong, while we ogled them, followed them – and, when they were out playing a match, went through their belongings with the maids. On one occasion, we found a condom – then called a French letter – much to Annie's glee. Of course, innocent me had no idea what it was. Or had I?

We exchanged looks and muffled laughter.

But for me these compulsory excursions to the Phoenix Park were tedious and humiliating. All those fielders at cover point, silly mid-on, square leg, the umpire, wrapped in discarded jerseys, the two men 'in' haring from one end of the pitch to the other, seeped into my subconscious. Apart from helping me in my old age to solve crossword puzzles, I could have done without this acquired knowledge. 'Howzat?!'

Religion

My religion – or lack of it – tortured me. I was dreadfully traumatised by my terrors of hell. My Confirmation was the worst experience of my life. Mary Hone sat on my bed the day before and asked me was I ready for it. And how, oh how, I wished to scream: 'No, no, no, Mummy, no!' But didn't dare. Our lessons in Catechism had a Dante-esque quality. They were conducted in the dark above St Anne's Church in Dawson Street. The Dean, a tall man in gaiters, would sit near me, and his hand would slowly stray under my skirt. Not daring to move, I'd stiffen, holding my breath. I knew instinctively that if I moved away, I'd be the sinner: I'd have been responsible for his prurient pokings.

Then he'd take us down, one by one, and make us kneel in front of him. 'What is your worst sin?' Unable to speak, I'd let the hard boards drive into my knees, knowing that my face must be swelling with mortification. Eventually, he'd wave me away impatiently and call for the next unfortunate victim.

Confirmation Day. A new dress, short, white. A leather-bound hymn book from my aunt!

Years later, seeing Edward Munch's famous picture *The Scream* reminded me of that awful day.

FRIENDS

By now I had to invent a different persona. The only people I got on with were the outsiders, the 'different' ones – as in my friendship with Joyce O'Reilly, the only Catholic then at Alexandra. This was my hope of salvation, of having any sort of personal life at all. So my mother never knew of my friendship with Joyce. In order to go out with her on Saturdays, I had to introduce a respectable Protestant specimen, a dentist's daughter from Fitzwilliam Square.

If we picked up a Dublin accent, we were told to 'speak properly'. Yes, the dentist's daughter became a stand-in. She did not say 'Bleedin' this' and 'Bleedin' that', did not say 'Fuck' and 'Shit', or ask you if a feller had ever given you a 'thrill'. And she did not go home to high tea of ham and salad in Drumcondra.

'She seems a nice girl,' my mother whined out of the side of her mouth, on meeting this solemn, unimaginative specimen.

Holidays, half-days, weekends, I worked in the stables. We roamed the point-to-points and country shows. We started a riding school to pay for the showjumpers, picking up cobs and ponies for a few pounds. Shivering children clinging to the ponies' manes were dragged to the Moor of Meath, usually by me. I groomed, mucked out and brought the animals to the blacksmith. The same Joe Breen pulled the bellows, thrusting the shoe into the furnace and, when it was red-hot, hammering it into shape. When he was satisfied, he'd pick up the horse's hoof and, holding it between his legs and his split leather apron, would try it for shape on the hoof, causing an attractive odour of burning hair to waft into his forge. If the shoe fitted, he'd plunge it into water, which hissed and steamed, and tacked it on to the hoof.

'Stand, you bugger, you!'

How could one not have a pash on this handsome man? (Boring as it was to hold the tiresome horse, which, often as not, trod on your foot.)

His business was brisk. Often one had to queue behind tufted farm horses, while your own animal fussed and fretted and was in a right sweat by the time your turn came round.

'Stand, you bugger, you!'

But running this school wasn't paying. We fought away the hay bills that crowded in from the local farmers, the oats and bran bills from Shackleton's Mills. We trundled circuitous routes to avoid the eyes of our creditors. The animals suffered from malnutrition. So badly, in fact, that one Miss X sent the NSPCA round to us. This was humiliating, to say the least. Also shameful. How we cursed her, the stringy bitch, with a face like the funnel of a drain. But of course something had to be done. Eventually, after my mother's death, we shared out her jewellery, some of which was quite valuable. My sister got the emerald snake and I got a very lovely locket made of diamonds set in gold. It's not hard to guess which got sold. And this went some way to pay off the still-outstanding bills. A hundred pounds from a jewellers in O'Connell Street. What wouldn't it be worth now!

But to go back to the handsome blacksmith, Joe Breen. My mother, on the trail of talent, got a notion. She ordered him to make fire-dogs for the drawing-room grate. These andirons still stand, like two inquisitive dachshunds, in the house where my

90

father died. She pulled strings to get him a stand in the RDS. Thereafter, he gave up shoeing horses, making wrought-iron gates and all kinds of fancy artefacts, ending up a rich man and bringing fame to the village of Leixlip.

SWITZERLAND

So that summer of 1938 we had worked non-stop with the horses. Soon it would be time to take up my scholarship; my Aunt Olive was to accompany me through London to put me on the Dover ferry. This was the year before the outbreak of World War II.

I look back on this generosity on the part of my aunt with gratitude. I know she had an old Victorian notion of fixing me up into ladyhood, having faith in my ability for languages and music – but underneath, I think she hoped for a quintessential metamorphosis in my character. She perhaps wanted me to lose my generally sloppy demeanour and turn into some sort of debutante. Alas, on that score, she put her money on the wrong girl! Paloma would have filled that bill nicely.

We took the mail boat to Holyhead, and then the train to London, where we stayed for a few days. I went to see Madame Tussauds, the Tower, and Westminster. She hopped around the British Museum and the National Gallery on her crutches. London, huge and exciting, left me laggard, and I was glad to be dispatched on the train to Neuchâtel in Switzerland.

Two demoiselles, clad in identical garb – dark-brown skirts, hip-length jackets and berets – met me at the station. One thin and one thick. And I was taken up a long hill and up hundreds of steps, at the top of which was the Pensionat Irena. The Swiss sun shone from a transparent sky, and below, the lake stretched out, dotted with little boats and their cut-out paper sails.

The fat demoiselle brought me to my room. This I must share with an English girl called Susan.

Susan, secure as a cushion, had undented flesh made of muscle. Her rolling breasts, undivided, bulged out of her cotton dress, on which were painted roses, like scabs. She was six foot tall.

'Isn't it lovely here?' I breathed, my happiness escalating into my throat.

'When I was a baby,' I continued, 'I dreamt I was a mongoose and everybody liked me because I killed rats and mice and snakes.'

She looked at me curiously. 'I hate it here,' she said. 'I want to go home.'

After tea, which consisted of bread and jam – no butter – we went for a march up the Jura Mountains with the thin Mademoiselle Dubois, striding ahead like a man. Needles underfoot, soft as sawdust; spokes of sunlight coming through the fir trees; a wispy breeze penetrating our frocks. I wanted to live like this forever and ever.

The Continental girls, especially the Yugoslavs, looked darkly aged. The Dutch were more bouncy but not as self-assured as the Germans, who had jutting Aryan chins and stomped around with their youth and strength a credit to the fatherland.

As usual, I was the odd one out. The only Irish girl, and one with a built-in talent for mischief-making, I circled the packs uncertainly.

We studied the nineteenth-century novelists and poets: Verlaine, Baudelaire:

Mon enfant, ma soeur, songe a la douceur,
D'aller là-bas, vivre ensemble.

My madness made me light-headed, my heart full of fire. One night, I persuaded some girls to buy bottles of Neuchâtel wine at a shilling a bottle, and I led them into the woods. There we broke the tops off and drank the wine through handkerchiefs. Roaring drunk – the glory of it – we roamed through tussocks, rocking with mirth and abandon. But like all my contretemps with the forbidden, I went too far. On returning to the house, I reeled against the Italian master, Senior Attilio. I threw my arms round him and kissed him on his sodden lips. He took little joy in these excesses, pushed me away; the sophisticated demoiselles laughed. I felt a fool and could never look him in the eye again. Again, I was nearly thrown out but was given the 'one more chance' routine.

Soon I became emotionally involved with another pupil, a Danish girl, Birgit Loft. We were both wild, strong, adventurous and athletic.

When the snow came, it brought a sudden silence. We crept out at night into the mountains, skied off into the moonlight, the trees flashing past: light, dark, dark, light. We cuddled together in the cabin under the big featherbeds like two puppies. Laughing, eating together, filled the caverns of my heart. It was enough. A breath of the idyll that seldom repeats itself.

War clouds gathered. The two big Germans sang songs of their fatherland:

Adieu mein kleine gard officier, Adieu,
Und vergis mich nicht, und vergis mich nicht.

Their blonde heads absorbing sunshine, they stomped around like athletes. Germany would win the next war; of this they were certain. It was June 1939. The Yugoslavs and Hungarians crouched more darkly. The English fretted and wanted to go home, and I thought only of my eventual leave-taking from Birgit. And I never wanted to go home. Never, never, never.

But her parents wanted her home. They wrote from Denmark. The day of our leave-taking is still very vivid in my memory. How we stood on the concrete veranda of the Pensionat, somewhat confused, our eyes dry, and then when a vehicle came for her, she simply went.

I mourned her loss, but I still exulted in my being there. We swam every day in the lake. Every hour I measured this lightness in me, which I knew would be taken from me when I went home. When the English girls talked of homesickness, I did not understand what they meant. One small, brown-eyed, cowering English girl became friendly with me. She spoke of her mother all the time: how much she loved her and how her mother was beaten every day by an alcoholic lover. When eventually we arrived at Victoria Station in London, there she was, a tiny lined creature, with dyed-red hair and violent lipstick, her pretty face battered with misery. They ran and held each other, two stricken creatures.

I crossed London and from Euston Station took the train to Holyhead. At Dun Laoghaire, my mother met me. Our faces bumped together.

She asked, 'What have you done with your eyebrows?'

I had done really well in my exams, got top marks in French literature, and my music teacher wrote glowingly of my work.

For what?

Suddenly, it was all for nothing. My education had been pulled down around me like a billowing tent.

I wanted to go to college. Out of the question. 'We've spent enough money on Noll and Paloma's education.'

There had been extreme difficulty in getting money from my mother when I was away. The English girl, Susan, had offered to sell me her dress – a long white satin, off-the-shoulder one – for a pound. I had to write three times for the money. It was quite soiled and ugly when I finally wore it but I flounced about in it as though it had been designed by a famous couturier. There are still letters from the demoiselles asking my mother for money for this and that, and getting negative replies. Only for my Aunt Olive, who paid the bills, I'd have been sent home long before, after my scholarship was up.

My brother had got a job in an oil company in Basra, and Paloma had just finished in the Ling gymnasium in Dublin learning to be a gym teacher. So there was I like a snowball, having gone through storms of emotion and achievement, turned back into an ugly brown lump.

The Emergency

On 3 September, in the drawing room of Leixlip House, a knot of people were poring over the wireless. Anthony Eden's sepulchral tones. The newscaster. Churchill. De Valera reassuring us. Lord Haw Haw. Alistair Cooke's 'Letter from America'.

The fire was inclined to smoke. My father knelt in the grate holding a paper against the flames. Eventually the paper caught and lacy pieces flew up the chimney.

My mother said, 'Leave it, Pat.'

She was thinner, her voice increasingly low. Her sideways presentation of speech more pronounced. She sat facing the window in her high-backed chair. She asked me to get her some Anadin.

She began to store things. Sugar, tea, flour. She looked much older but kept on fussing about shortages. I did messages. Ran hither and thither; mostly got in the way. She was getting weaker and weaker, although she insisted on riding to the hunt once a week. She decided also that one of us should learn German in case they won the war! So I was dispatched once a week to a top flat in Fitzwilliam Square, where a German refugee was hiding over my Uncle Bob's surgery and residence. This delighted me not only for the chance to learn a new European language but also for the tea and cake that this sad thin lady provided. I can't have attended many lessons because I didn't learn much, nor can

I remember her name, although I have a misty memory of a lemon-coloured linen suit she always wore. Looking back on it, I imagine it must have broken my mother's heart to have to part with any more money for my education – not to mention my bus fare! Indeed, maybe the poor woman didn't get paid and, like Aiyuni, had to work for her keep.

Leaves began to drop, nights grew longer, rain ran down the drainpipes and bubbled into the gulleys. October turned in grey and drear, and during that winter she decided to advertise for paying guests.

And on a wet wintry day, a woman drove up in an Alvis sports car.

This was Evelyn Townshend.

These strange people, who came and went, were known as 'PGs' (for 'paying guests'). I suppose because of my mother's latent snobbery, this sounded better than saying she ran a boarding house. Some years previous to this, the poet Katherine Tynan and her daughter Pamela Hinkson had stayed with us for a while. They both occupied the same room – across the landing from mine. What was most distinctive about them was their hair. It was very scarce, and they spent hours brushing each other's hair. They were pleasant and would entertain me in their room late at night for a cup of Horlicks. I had no idea how highly thought of Katherine Tynan was. To me, she was just another ancient in a long black dress, while her daughter; Pamela, puffed away at her novels. So, compared with them, this woman, Miss Townshend, was full of oxygen and energy.

The Pilot

Yes, Miss Townshend, a high-speed woman around thirty-five, informed us that she also had a horse and an aeroplane. It was a Gypsy Moth, and she had parked it in Collinstown, where the airport was under construction.

Where she came from and where she went eventually, I do not know. Nor do I know where she got her money. The plane, the limousine, the thoroughbred bay – some eighteen hands high – how did they get there? Was it like the fox and the geese and the bag of meal? Did she bring one and go back for the rest? I do know that she had broken international law by flying a plane during the Emergency.

With a figure like a teenage boy, and a cynical know-all expression, it was soon clear that she had no time for my mother. Nor did she like Paloma. They glared at each other like two geese.

She took over the house.

But mother was intrigued. Was her name not 'Townshend'? Had she not originally come from Cork? She must be related to Somerville and Ross, my mother's heroines. But Miss Townshend, eventually 'Evelyn', shrugged this off.

'Why doesn't she care about this,' mother whined.

She had no time for such literary speculation, although she admitted to being part of a branch of the family, and she and my mother became more and more distant. She would brush past her on the stairs as though she owned the place.

Since the start of the Emergency, all private flying had been suspended. But she wanted to get her B licence, which needed practice and study. She went to see de Valera. Nobody we'd ever known had been to see Dev. But with her extraordinary powers of persuasion, he listened to her, and eventually gave her permission to fly – but within a stringently defined area.

She singled me out as a willing amanuensis. At night in her room, I sat with her ledgers on my knee, asking her pertinent questions about aerodynamics and higher mathematics. During the day, we'd speed to Collinstown, racing other cars, driving on the pavements, and there she'd hitch herself into her gear and, with me beside her, we'd hedge-hop over the flat fields of Swords, the Naul, and Howth. Round and round we'd circle, while I interrogated her, keenly correcting her if she made a mistake.

Still I begged to be let go to Trinity.

'No. You must stay at home and look after things.'

So I looked after things.

1940, 1941, bombs fell on another island. We listened to the news. Lord Haw Haw's 'Gairmany Calling, Gairmany Calling'. Alistair Cooke, whose voice came in waves across the Atlantic. English and German airmen crashed around the country and ended up in the Curragh. They were treated very well, especially the English, who only had to clock in at night. When our riding school got going, a tall, mannered man turned up on the doorstep inquiring about hiring a horse. For a while, he kept his name secret, but he eventually admitted that he was one of the English airmen who was 'staying' at the camp. He seemed to have plenty of money and often took us to the pictures. Then there was the North Strand bomb. We ran up the hill to watch the conflagration. We stood on each other's shoulders, our hearts thumping with excitement.

Mother and I went to first-aid classes in the village and Father joined the ARP. Later I did six weeks in a Dublin hospital as part of a home-nursing course. (This was a frightening experience, which is why I do not wish to name the hospital.) I worked in a 'surgical' ward of about fifteen beds. I made beds, scrubbed floors and sluiced out filthy sheets in an adjacent corridor given over to the laundry. The treatment in general was merely trying to keep the patients clean, without even the most primitive additions, like toilet paper. We had to use towels to wipe the patients' bottoms. I particularly remember one young man whose bedsores were great craters of hanging flesh. He had broken his back when a tree he was cutting fell on him. When I asked the nurse how could she bear to tend to him so patiently when he must be in such pain, she reassured me that he couldn't feel it because 'his nerves were numb'. My heart was torn asunder for these poor people suffering, as they must have done. I gladly did messages for them, with daily excursions for cigarettes. Everyone smoked – not only the patients, but also the doctors and nurses. And because of everyone's inherent good humour – both men and women – working among them was made bearable. I ended up getting so fond of both patients and nurses that I missed them when my six-week stint ended.

Of course the dreadful, primitive conditions in the hospital had little or nothing to do with the war: they were simply one of the many manifestations of the rampant poverty all over Ireland, and most obviously in the cities, during those early-twentieth-century decades. Children with shoes were a rare sight. Every evening at four, small boys would race to the offices of the *Evening Herald* and *Evening Mail* to collect their bundles of papers, with the potential profit of a halfpenny for ten papers sold. They would shout 'Hegla mail! Hegla mail!' These are simply my highlights of the Emergency as the war years unpeeled – for example my doing a course in First Aid and Home Nursing.

What upset us most was the inability to move. For instance, I would have loved to go to Paris, where I believed all art began and ended. But England was the only place we could go to, and of course very many went to work there. But life for us continued, with very little change. Shortages of tea and coffee seemed to be the worst miseries we encountered, mitigated by the sheets of 'penny poems' I used to love buying on the streets of Dublin.

> Bless 'em all, Bless 'em all
> The long and the short and the tall
> Bless de Valera and Sean McEntee
> They promised to give us the half-ounce of tea.

Etc! (These, of course, were brought back to me most vividly when I much later read James Joyce's *Pomes Penyeach*.) Also, of course, the shortage of petrol. This brought out many ingenious substitutes. There was the gasbag on the roof of the car, which in some way was hitched up to supply the engine with power. There was also a kind of steam-fired stove fed by two furnaces at the back of the vehicle. However, in spite of these few setbacks, many soldiers came over from England on leave to eat well and buy clothes. There's no doubt that Dev was a clever man to keep us out of the war but, as I've said, and everyone knows, Ireland was in a severe state of economic decline, with poverty and ill health the norm for the majority of citizens. It was not until the mid-forties that, because of Noël Browne's insistence on the building of new sanatoria, the scourge of TB was somewhat abated. But for the middle classes, like ourselves, with plenty of vegetables and fruit, and meat easy to get, compared with similar English people, we lived like kings. There was also very little change in our activities: the North Kildare Harriers continued to meet, and now, with our heterogeneous collections of nags, I followed the hunt like the rest of them.

PAIN

Mother and I rode out to the meet, which was in Moyvalley. I now had to watch her. She rode loosely; she had lost her original sang-froid. This irked me, of course. I wanted to be away in front of the field but had to straggle along at the tail, keeping an eye on her. Coming to a narrow dip in the ground, her mare stumbled, then righted itself. My mother screamed. A tortured, long-drawn-out scream. 'Help me! Help me! I've broken my neck!'

She was still on the horse, so I led her gingerly out on to the road and slowly we got to Maynooth. Here I telephoned home, and Tom arrived in the car to collect her.

Of course, mean as I was, I didn't believe she was really hurt, and later that evening as she lay in bed, pitifully weeping, I still thought she was overdoing it. I had always imagined that you died immediately if your neck was broken. I was heartless and efficient, ran hither and thither, phoning my Uncle Bob, seeing to things.

That night, she was taken into the Meath Hospital.

Yes, she had indeed broken a vertebra in her neck. So they strung her up. She must sit up all night suspended by pulleys fastened to her skull, lest the fractured bone sever her spinal chord.

She sat two days and two nights without sleep. Pain walked, stalked the wards, the road to Dublin, the corridors of the hospital. We lived with her pain until the pain forgot us and she had to shelter it alone, hold it in her arms, cradle it.

From now on, it was her pain that dominated the house. Out of hospital, she wore a high yellow collar, still dressing in her tussores and silks, her angora cardigans, her pleated skirts. She walked slowly, sat always in the high-backed chair, and I fetched the Anadin.

Evelyn continued to ignore these details, impatiently progressing with her studies, in spite of the darkness that had settled over the place.

My father continued to make stylish furniture, cursing the mass production practised by factories in the city, where they undercut his prices with inferior goods. His accounts never balanced. Occasionally, I helped him add up the figures. Dagg's lorry was a perpetual headache. He had been lent money and he was always behind on the repayments.

'The books would balance if it weren't for Dagg's lorry,' my father grumbled – not without humour. Then the factory went on fire.

Yes, the Leixlip Woodworking Company was burned to the ground. All the imported timber – mahogany, Austrian oak and deal – went up like tinder. The corrugated-iron roof, curled, lifted and crashed to the ground. Flames rose above the trees, above the village street. The village woke up to make a human rope of buckets from the pump. The Dublin Fire Brigade turned back at the Liffey bridge: Leixlip was in Kildare, out of its jurisdiction. We should have sent to Naas. By the time they arrived, the place was gutted, machines twisted, a tragic sculpture amongst the smoldering remains. The inlaid tables, the chairs, the dressers, the beds a heap of ash.

A man's heart breaks easily. My father, in his carpet slippers, kicked at a girder. He thanked the people of Leixlip for having done their best and walked slowly up the hill. Mother tried to comfort him, sick as she was. In a poem I wrote years later for my father, I mentioned how my mother said to him, as he kicked at the remains: 'If you do that, you'll burn your boots as well.'

In the kitchen, we drank bottled coffee. 'Irel' was the trade name of this noxious liquid, mother's mouth a scar of bewilderment. Nobody spoke.

Not only I wondered. Had Johnny Byrne taken his revenge? No one mentioned arson, but the word hung in the air. It was easier to think that one of the cabinetmakers had left a cigarette smouldering in the sawdust. Casually cast away, half stamped out.

Wood could no longer be imported, native timber was hard to season. Sycamore and cedar warped, the veneers lifted off. Although he rebuilt the factory, his heart wasn't in it, and it wasn't till much later that Barney Heron took it over, installed a kiln and made wooden houses.

Now father had to restore his equilibrium, take stock. His wife getting more feeble every day, his chief interest gone – apart from cricket, which he still took pleasure in. He took to gardening in a frenzied manner. We had a good orchard of Coxes, and these he carefully pruned; with my help, he sorted and laid them out. Every week, he'd go to the market with them. Whatever he did, he did professionally. Mother did her best, lost in her dying. She wrote letters to Noll, to her brothers in England. Jack was in the land army. Maurice, too old for the draft, lived comfortably in Maidenhead. Her younger brother, Bob, continued to work in the Rotunda and the Children's Hospital. He was chiefly concerned with the dreadful poverty in Dublin, and instigated the Bewley's Fund, where families could come and be fed. It wasn't easy, as the Catholic Hierarchy, under the aegis of Archbishop McQuaid, claimed it was more important for the children's souls to be looked after, and that a crucifix should hang over their beds, than that their bodies should be adequately fed and housed. Later, Bob applied for a job in the new maternity hospital in the Coombe and was turned down for being a Protestant.

My grandparents and my Aunt Olive and Uncle Joe Hone still visited from time to time. And I escaped with Evelyn as often as I could.

Pain attacked my mother at every moment of the day. Every bone in her body was on fire. Analgesics piled up in the medicine chest. My father put the rug over her knees and I fetched the painkiller. At night, we'd sit round the dining-room stove, roasting our shins or in the kitchen, tiptoeing round like thieves. The cold in the house was always unbearable, dirt collected in the crevices. Rose was mother's helpmeet. A truly saintly person, she had had TB and, thanks to Noël Browne's new sanatoria, had been cured. She cared for Mother as though she were her own child.

'God help her,' she'd say, 'she'd be better off . . . '

A thought we shared but never mouthed.

She called for the priest. During those last few years, she had toyed with the idea of becoming a Catholic. She had begun to take instruction. Perhaps she, too, found the chill of Protestantism of no comfort. Since her sister Joyce had long been a Catholic, she may have had some encouragement from her. The priest came and went; his prayers hummed in the room like a swarm of bees.

However, although she said she wished to be buried in the Catholic graveyard, she must have lost heart or patience, because she stayed to the end as a member of the Church of Ireland.

Nineteen forty, Evelyn still there, flying her Gypsy Moth, driving her Alvis, riding her horse.

I cut pictures of Paloma out of the *Irish Times*. Paloma getting a red rosette in Ballinasloe, in the RDS. We started a camogie team in the village. Paloma went to the Salmon Leap Inn and drank whiskey. Mrs Colgan, the owner, disapproved of us. 'Two straps.'

I wanted to go to Trinity.

'Why on earth?' asked Paloma.

Along with petrol rationing, there was a scarcity of coal, so the trains ran largely on turf. Dev insisted the country grow more wheat. There were mountains of turf in the Phoenix Park; the polo ground was ploughed for potatoes. Evelyn Townshend and I sailed over the hinterland in her plane.

Mother mourned the absence of her son.

Mother was dying now, we knew, though she still limped about, sat in the high chair. I fetched the Anadin.

Mother did not want to die.

What hovered in the corners of her mind?

Did she ever think of those letters of all those years ago? When she was a young attractive woman. In love. Writing back daily to her beloved in the trenches? Running to the postman to get his letters?

My Dearest, did you ever get a letter from me written by the moonlight. This is one. A very long day has brought me to the desolate and famous spot. In charge of a 'little fatigue party', I have just got a tent. I didn't expect it, thought I should be sleeping in the open. It feels rather like a picnic or a return to Canada. The snow is on the ground yet the air is mild. This is miserable moonlight. I don't know when this will get to you. Good night dear, am sitting on my tin hat, a good seat . . .

I wonder will I get any shamrock for the 17th. Probably not as the post is so slow . . . There is a strange little cat comes into the mess. The place is full of rats. That was partly why I went on top. I am not nerve-broken except for the rats, and it is quite serious as I cannot sleep at all when they come in and screech at night . . .

Then she couldn't get up any more. My Uncle Bob gave Paloma and me instructions. A silver syringe. A collection of needles. A little silver case. A spoon. Methylated spirits. A sixth of a grain of morphine to be given to her every four hours. Intramuscular.

Every other night, we took it in turns to lie behind the Indian screen on the settle bed. When Mother groaned, we emptied the ampoule from the phial on to the spoon and added water. After drawing the mixture into the syringe, we cleared out the air.

I stood at the winter window. 'I want to go to college' was my boring leitmotif.

'You'll make a man happy one day,' Mother said, her voice far away on the horizons of our thoughts.

I looked over at the bed. Who was she addressing? We didn't ask.

She began asking for an overdose. Suffering and pain became separate from my mother's person. We lived in fear of it.

Dearest, a very nice dog has attached himself to us. A very big red setter of moderate age, very sad and rather thin, but we have just fed him and hope he will stay. He drank about 1 gal. of water. I have made him a bed in this dugout. He shows a little interest in the rats. His name is Pincher, christened by Wilkey . . .

Rats.

Like trying to get out of an uncomfortable garment, we began to work our lives round it. The pain. We squealed as we filled the syringes, squirting water at each other, ducking, helpless with giggles.

We crept out when we could. Went to the Salmon Leap Inn. Paloma met new boys.

The pond in Phoenix Park froze over. We went skating there, twisting and waltzing as though we'd done it all our lives. We turned our heads when we gave the injections. Rose helped her with her toiletry, holding the bedpan, her hand on my mother's lower abdomen. When a little water trickled out, Rose said: 'That's better.'

Bones were boiled down in the kitchen. The marrow extracted. A little marrow would be spooned between the parched lips. Sometimes she took some Brands Essence.

In the dining room, we ate like pigs, wiping our mouths on the backs of our hands. We tripped over the dogs on our rush back to the sickroom. We learnt which stair creaked – to be avoided so as not to disturb.

The long dark days continued. Summer scattered into autumn, autumn into winter. The tall house swayed in the wind, rain beat on the windowpanes, ran into the shores.

And the memory of that terrible war. Did my father think back to those days of courtship as he saw his wife now, as he stroked her forehead, where Rose had sprayed the lavender water?

All the letters she had so carefully kept.

Dearest, (Christmas Day.) . . . The men are awfully good and work in the most cheerful way, Sundays and today. They didn't get their Christmas dinner till dark. . . . My love to you this Christmas night and may it be the last in this place and away from you. Love, Darling, Pat. Champagne is drunk tonight in the mess.

And twenty-odd years after she had received that letter, it was Christmas Day again. There was no wine. No crackers. No charades.

In April 1941, my mother died.

A few days, maybe a week, before, two starched nurses had come. Dressed like swans, they bustled about. The house became different, cleaner. The nurses expected extensive hygiene, regular meals, spotless rooms of their own. We ran about, waiting on them. They were so big, with their winged caps and crackling garments. We stood with our backs to the window, with nothing to do.

Mother called Pat from time to time, her frail tones hovering in the air. He was gentle. Of no consequence. It was hell for him. We didn't notice. He was invisible. The nurses ate the oxygen.

Released from our vigil, we slept in our own room, plummeting into an unconscious abyss till the night the breathing began.

It was slow. It crescendoed, the walls expanded. In my head, the Sonata – B flat minor. I slept, I woke. Lento, again lento.

I shivered beneath the sheets, terrified, my head under the pillow, my hands clutching the pillowcase. Death approaching, staying away. Death hovering, the walls echoing.

At eight in the morning, my father entered the room. 'Your mother has passed away.'

I sat in my room, looking out over the soaking fields, the mutes, the black motor hearse, the cortège walking up the long road to the bridge over the Royal Canal, and on, stopping at the gates of the Catholic graveyard at Confey. Grandma, Grandpa, my stalwart Aunt Olive and her husband George, Uncle Bob Collis. Old Willy Collis wept in the cold wind, his red eyes streaming. His back bent with grief. He was perhaps the only one who still really loved my mother, Mary Hone, née Collis, his daughter.

They all clustered round the silver coffee pot, rubbed their hands at the fire. The mud was walked into the green carpet. The carpet so tastefully chosen by my mother. And I sat in my room till Evelyn came. She had come up to my room to tell me: 'Now is your time to get away.'

I looked at her, the stranger, the sprinting woman, the pilot, the sports-car driver, the horsewoman.

'What will we do with the dogs?'

'Leave.'

'Did you notice Daddy and Paloma crying in the church? They held on to each other.'

'And you sat alone.'

'I don't mean that.'

'I know what you mean.'

'No you don't.'

'Leave.'

I didn't know why I was angry with her. Just then, she knew more about me than I knew about myself. In this stunned, emotionless condition, I just stared out of the window.

So what had happened between my parents during those twenty-odd years between the end of the First World War and the year my mother died? Those terrible years in the trenches, about which we children knew nothing: did they radically change my father's outlook on life? Or was it my mother's rigidly bigoted outlook that took him away from his seemingly radical thinking, which surfaces from time to time in his letters? In those days, nobody spoke of 'post-traumatic stress disorder'.

Rats, unspeakable cold, terror. How can a man survive four years of this and be the same man after as before?

So there was my father, a man with whom I was a stranger. A man whom my mother had prevented me – and to a lesser extent Paloma – from knowing, left with the two of us, to muddle along in a morass of misunderstanding and bewilderment.

Evelyn stayed on in the house. I went to Miss Galway's secretarial college in Dawson Street. Father wouldn't give me the bus fare, so I cycled in and out of Dublin every day. I hung out of

Shackletons' steam lorry going up Lucan Hill. My bike a Rudge Whitworth, which had cost my father five pounds.

'I have to learn something,' I said.

Now Evelyn collected me in the afternoons and we resumed our jaunts in the air, bringing the plane down under my instructions, putting it into the hangar and speeding home in the Alvis, over and up.

Other days, I hung around Robert Roberts in Grafton Street, eyeing the UCD boys, smoking. In those days, you got a cigarette in the saucer of your cup. And this we gratefully smoked. And then back the long miles home, up over the Hermitage, past the Dead Man Murray's, the journey marked by those heart-scalding hills.

Skidding in the tramlines, tearing your stockings. Taunted by youths.

In Roberts, the two ladies at the piano and cello played Brahms's *Lullaby* pizzicato, their iron-grey skulls inclined over their instruments. We plastered our faces with lipstick and eye shadow, loitering, as usual, in Woolworth's, putting off the journey home for as long as possible.

Paloma accumulated boyfriends, attended the shows.

Father fumed, unable to handle us. He was very unhappy: Mother had propped him up against family problems. He hid himself in the garden, played cricket or golf at the weekends. Sometimes he went to Dublin to visit a lady friend, Una Moran. Mary Power and Cyril moved into the wing. Cyril worked in Jeyes Fluid. Was a golf partner for my father. Mary was from Limerick and had a grand accent, rode out to hounds on a tall chestnut, made friends with Paloma. I kept my distance.

These gap years, between my mother's dying and Paloma's finally leaving, in retrospect seem to have been in some strange way welded together. They were mostly marked by lack of money, ever-increasing inability to pay the fodder bills. Traipsing around with Paloma's horsy coterie. A Swiss undergraduate, originally from Limerick, took a fancy to me and we had a wishy-washy relationship. We more or less did what we liked. Father had given up on us, I suppose. Young women occasionally came out to Leixlip to help us with the horses. But there is in my memory an aura of searching in a void, a day-to-day existence that was getting us nowhere. We never really thought of this in relation to Mother's being no longer there, with her strictures and her social needs and her dominating personality and, yes, her desperateness. It was a bit like being dried up after a heavy storm: the aridity dehydrated the spirit.

Father had never really been in charge. He couldn't cope with responsibility. When he got angry, he just railed. To go right back to his beginnings, he'd been run by women. His elder sister Olive – my aunt – had been his first prop. In her eyes, he could do no wrong. One of her repeated words of doom was 'You'll never find a man as wonderful as your father to marry' – a prognosis that made me secretly cynical. Then, of course, after the war, came my mother, who maybe spoiled him even more determinedly. For this reason, probably, he was no good as the boss of the woodworking factory. When things went wrong – as in the case of the Byrne child, already alluded to – he couldn't handle it: his inhuman attitude was all part of his not being able to cope with these kind of emotional setbacks on his own, just as when any of our bad or wild behaviour came to his notice. So naturally, to avoid his outbursts of temper, we lied and hid from him as much as possible.

However, in spite of this, Paloma and I still spent a great deal of time enjoying ourselves. If there was a dance in a marquee, we'd cycle off, myself on the crossbar – even as far as Kilcock.

On one occasion, we went to a dance in Carton House, which had been taken over by the Irish army. The officers were handsome and stupid in their khaki uniforms. They had burned a goodly portion of this magnificent house with schoolboy pranks. We misinterpreted them. Thought one of them might fall in love with one of us. This unfortunately had far-reaching results – more of which later.

I don't know about Paloma, but I couldn't release myself from the trauma of that last year of my mother's illness. Every night, I dreamed of her in the coffin. She was always scratching at the lid, trying to get out, her hands transparent as tissue paper. By day, my mind was blackened by the memory of those hours of the Cheyne-Stokes breathing. Years later, I read in D. H. Lawrence's *Sons and Lovers* the exact description of this when his own mother was dying, and this helped me somewhat. I was not the only one to have to carry the guilty burden of this memory.

But I do remember swearing to myself that if ever I had children, I would never allow them to go through a similar experience.

Spring fell into summer, and then there was 'the man in the loft'.

PALOMA AGAIN

John Price lived with his mother and retarded sister in a leaking farmhouse in Westmeath surrounded by poor land, mostly bog. John Price of the high cheekbones, split teeth and doe eyes. With the square frame and laughing mouth. He came to live with Paloma in the loft above the yard. The stables ringed the back of the yard. The long loft above ended in chipped stone steps giving on to the cobbles. At the back of the loft was an opening with a ladder, facing out on to the top yard, with its ever-increasing piles of horse and cow shit.

John loved Paloma, simply. He'd bite his underlip with his split teeth and smile at me – the sister, Childe.

I lived on a cliff edge of anxiety while they sucked stout from the necks of bottles, threw cigarette butts into the dregs. At night, they'd come into the kitchen and cook fries while I kept *cave* at the door. Paloma seemed to think it the most natural thing in the world to keep a 'fancy man' in the loft without my father's knowing.

Now John accompanied us to the point-to-points, the shows. We loaded the horses on to the goods train at Leixlip and the train puffed away at a deathly slow pace. We often stopped in the middle of nowhere to have the engine replenished with turf. Always short of money, I rode in the horsebox, sitting under the horses' legs in the straw. We went to Ballinasloe, where

I was promised a ride on a large bay, recently acquired. A fairly unreliable animal but a splendid jumper when he felt like it. However, at the last moment she decided that John should have the ride, and I got drunk with annoyance.

In Ballinasloe, there were all the trappings of the old hiring fairs. Girls were still sold at the corners, and the pavements were awash with Guinness. A man would bid, and the father of the girl would throw in a couple of heifers. They haggled and spat on their hands. Large farm horses were bought and sold, and there was always the showjumping as the pièce de résistance.

I was already a drinker, as I have said, and one of the nights I tottered into bed, only to wake up beside a bald lady. Apart from that adventure, I spent most of the time in the stables grooming and mucking out.

Then, late that summer, she had to tell us. She couldn't hide it any longer: the unfastened breeches, the expanded breasts.

Uncle Bob – as usual the family mentor – was consulted. Aunt Olive stepped in and it was arranged for herself and John to be sent to a cottage in County Cork to live as man and wife until the child was born and a nice family found to bring it up. Uncle Bob would see to this.

Father prowled about in agony. 'Remember Patsy' was said. Patsy Cooper had had a baby which died at birth. I cowered into myself. Obsessively inhibited like my mother on the one hand, and smug on the other, I awaited events.

I had a real terror of sex. It had been beaten into me by my mother's psychological abstractions. Indeed, when we had been learning first aid, when she was asked to point out her pelvis, my mother was unable to do so. The teacher lost her temper and threw my mother's hand on her mount of Venus, saying to the others in the class: 'Did you ever!'

Of course I longed for love and kisses, as I had since I was twelve years old. But I was too ugly, I knew, to attract a boy. Paloma's cast-offs would have died rather than kiss me.

116

I finished up at Miss Galway's, having spent most of the time in the lavatory reading Chekhov's short stories with Maureen, who later became Cyril Cusack's wife. 'The Lady with the Toy Dog'.

So now I was thrown into the sole company of my father. He had loved and admired Paloma so much and could not be expected to communicate with me. I mooched about listlessly, collecting the windfalls for the village women, who came with their sacks. Sixpence filled a sack. And as before, I sorted and shelved the Coxes, the Worcester pearmains and the large cooking apples. As usual I had no money, till eventually father decided to give me an allowance of twenty-one shillings a month. When the month was up, I had to follow him up and down stairs or into his office and literally beg for it. This money all went on fags. Ticked up and paid off every four weeks.

There was still the remnants of our riding school. And on one occasion, my Uncle Bob asked me to bring a pony to Calary for his young sons to ride. Riding a bay horse called Davy, I led a pony – a grey, somewhat obstinate animal called Silver – all the way from Leixlip to Calary bog. The journey – some seven or eight hours – turned out to be a bit of a waste of time. Silver wouldn't do anything the boys wanted, and the youngest, Robbie – who really enjoyed riding – was very frustrated. My uncle put such store by physical prowess that he could be impatient with his sons, and the whole trip ended in tears. So in this somewhat disjointed fashion, I stayed on at Leixlip, teaching the few kids who straggled out – little boys, mostly, whose fathers wanted to 'toughen them up' – on this recalcitrant grey.

Luckily, I had one friend, whom I'd met in Dublin. Aileen Monson. Whenever possible, she came to stay with me, or I went to stay with her, in a ramshackle house on the Swords road. Through her, I met others, including Diarmuid Ó Ceaillaigh, son of the Irish professor in UCD. Somehow or other, we managed to go to dances occasionally. It was a pound in. This was an impossible sum to accumulate, so we developed a trick which meant that we could get into the Metropole for nothing. If you ran fast enough upstairs to leave your coat, the doorman would assume that you had already paid in, and you'd stroll into the ballroom, head in the air. There was another friend of Aileen's, a floorwalker in Switzers, so that made up our dancing foursome.

Never having any clothes, I yanked the curtains off one of the windows and made myself a kind of Grecian garment. Dermot, in the same boat, would have to get his suit out of pawn.

We would steal his father's car by pushing it down the road for half a mile before starting the engine, and then away we'd sail like millionaires. We were great mates. Once we dressed up in similar clothes and called at the Sailor's Relief Fund place, asking to sign on board a ship, saying we were brother and sister. But they sent us packing.

We'd go camping in Portrane, courtesy of Evelyn, who dumped us there in her Alvis.

Evelyn was now, surprisingly, going out with a neighbour in Celbridge. Heavily married he was, and this created mayhem. He owned point-to-point horses and she took her horse over to his stables. I was occasionally asked to ride one or other of his horses in the gallops at Baldonnel, where there was a good straight run. But I missed her friendship and approval – the first I'd ever had from an adult, apart from my Aunt Olive.

Paloma had the baby in the Rotunda and nobody ever saw him. (We were told he was a boy, although years later it was found to be a girl, as the daughter traced her lineage. I was the only one who knew who the child's father was: the event had indeed happened that fatal night of the dance at Carton House!) She and John got married in St Douglas Church on the Malahide road, my Aunt Olive holding the reception, and they went to live in Westmeath, in John's inhospitable farmhouse.

The gap of years now closed, the occupants of Leixlip House dwindled to two Hones and the aforementioned Myra, the wonderful soprano. A not-very-comfortable trio.

LOVE

That summer, something happened that influenced the next fifteen years of my life – and indeed changed the whole current of my ambitions.

My Aunt Olive, in her old-fashioned way, imagined that upper-class young ladies should meet similar young men. She had an Austen-esque belief in this. For this reason, she gave tennis parties, inviting all the eligible young bachelors along. The Jamesons, and suchlike. She didn't seem to realise how schizophrenic I was – how, to survive, I must lead a dual existence. Nor did she see how ugly I still thought I was. Although I had shed the puppy fat and was lean as a stick, my head was as big as a rugby ball. Young fellows like their girls to be beautiful.

However, I now played a mean game of tennis, with a riveting serve and a cunning backhand. At one of these tennis parties, I met Christopher Cooper. He was my father's first cousin, some twenty years older than me: forty-odd to my twenty.

Something happened to me. I felt as if the ground had shifted. We went hunting lost balls in the shrubbery. He was so beautiful, in his open shirt and with his careless arms. My movements blurred into each other, my blood rose like mercury.

As we sat on the sidelines later, he asked: 'Do you like films?'

I showed him my legs, long and shapely. 'Yes,' I said.

A few nights later, we went to the pictures. The Marx Brothers' *Day at the Races*. Sometimes our bare arms brushed each other as we rocked in our seats, and we doubled up in helpless laughter.

On Aston Quay, as I waited for the last bus, we leant over the Liffey wall. The brackish water swirled beneath us, the lights reflected like blobs of oil, and he said, oh so casually: 'Perhaps we should get married.' The bus came, and I jumped aboard. The following day he went back to England, taking all of himself with him: his loose arms, his domed forehead, his crooked laughing mouth, his rich black eyebrows.

THE COOPERS

This family had influenced my childhood.

Aiyuni, as I've said, taught me all I knew in the way of education. After she got her degree, she worked in the Eye and Ear Hospital in Adelaide Road as an almoner. In those days, almoners were the people on whom the poor of Dublin relied to have their families treated in the hospitals without paying. A session with the almoner was intimidating. You had to prove you were more or less penniless to get free (or, for that matter, *any*) treatment. Then there was Patsy. She, unlike her sister, was breezy. As time went on, and it was pretty sure she'd marry Charles, she became even more buoyant. Unfortunately, she had very bad eyesight. Great luminous brown eyes that blinked all the time. It was miraculous that she was able to do such close work in the factory. (The fact that she had once had a baby was unknown to us then.) Unlike Aiyuni, she had no ambition to go to college. There were also two other sisters, Grace and Honour, and one brother, John, who later married Nancy Starkie, sister of the notorious Enid, flamboyant Oxford academic and biographer of Baudelaire, amongst others.

So they all came from the same stem, my father's mother having been Sarah Cooper before she married William Hone.

And all that previous generation grew up in Cooper Hill in the nineteenth century: a formidable mansion in County Clare, near Limerick. Formidable it was in many ways: damp, freezing and tumbling down. There were eighteen in the family, the father having married twice, his first wife having died, I imagine, from TB. Apparently in the adjoining village, people would say how strange it was that so many of those in the neighbourhood resembled the old man! They were said to be as beautiful as they were poor, the boys going barefoot, and the girls only having one ball dress between them. And there again, there is a strange tale. Apparently their father had changed his name from 'Tuthill' to 'Cooper' to please his godmother. The Coopers – blessed, as they were, with brains and beauty – nevertheless must have been a profligate lot: they were always said to be much better at spending money than earning it. They could trace themselves back to Maire Ruadh O'Brien, who had married one Ensign Cooper in the sixteenth century in order to keep her lands for her son. A wild woman, who, it is said, soon grew tired of her husband and pointed Cooper's horse in the direction of the Cliffs of Moher. But this must have been after he had sired another son, which began this rackety dynasty in Ireland. (The ruins of her castle, Leamaneh Castle, still stand.)

Old Robert Cooper, the father of Patsy and Aiyuni, had been in the merchant navy. And when I was a child, he and his wife lived in Monasterevin. Occasionally I stayed there, and it was joyful. Everyone streeled around in their nightclothes, uninhibited by strictures or reprimands. Penniless, like his forebears, the old man was gently eccentric, and one loved him dearly.

So now here comes Christopher. Another branch of the same exhaustive tree.

Just then, having been living in England, he was called up into the forces. He got a job in intelligence. (He was a Slavonic scholar and a friend of Hubert Butler's – they had taken the same degree in London University.) His job – which bored him stiff – was, as he put it, teaching Poles to teach Poles to teach English. And there was I, without a pick of education apart from my burgeoning love of books and my brief flirtation with French literature, falling lock, stock and barrel for this witty – and, to me, extraordinary – man.

CAVAN

Two weeks later, Paloma rang me up. 'Do you want a job in Cavan? Lord Farnham is looking for a groom who can ride the showjumpers and teach the grandchildren to ride.'

> *The garden of Eden has vanished, they say,*
> *But I know the lie of it still.*
> *And I'll take you down to the Bridge of Finay,*
> *And I'll bring you back to Cootehill.*

In the annual Cavan tennis tournament, I won the women's singles with a handicap of minus forty. In the rain. That night, the young players from Dublin gathered. We drank brandy and sang.

There was one young man, a Roman god with locks curling at the nape of his neck. I edged along the counter, pushed away the silky girls, touched his drink, ran my hand down the back of his bare arm. My bra strap fell down over my shoulder from under my sleeveless tennis frock. He was aware, unaware. I was in love with Christopher. We had written to each other, casual notes, my own with scratchings out and stupid stories, his short and pithy: *darling*, sometimes *dearest*. I edged nearer and nearer to the young Roman god. It grew late. I was very drunk. I ran to the lavatory, vomited and vomited. I ran along to the corridor, found an empty room, slept and woke and ran again. Ran till I found him, gorgeous in his bed. I jumped in beside him and he came on top of me between my legs, his penis barely touching my vagina, and I came from head to toe and toe to head, swirling and writhing, carried high on to a plane of pure pleasure from which I wished never to descend.

Quickly I ran again, ran downstairs, ran out into the yard, got on my bike and pedalled, pedalled, till I reached the gates of Farnham. There stood the lord's grandson.

'Don't tell, don't tell, don't tell.'

PART THREE

FARNHAM HOUSE

9th Jan 1916

My dearest Mary . . .

I am beginning another letter now as the supply of green envelopes is running short. I have just got your nice parcel. I thank you very much for it, dear. The honey is very good. Never surely did soldiers live in such luxury as we do. I got a book on Æ by Darrel Figgis from home the other day. I didn't think much of it except for a grand attack quoted in it by Æ against Rudyard Kipling, occupying three pages or more. R.K. apparently had been throwing mud at the Irish Nationalists. I can only remember the line something like, 'You have belittled my country, you who have no country but only an empty empire to roam in . . . '. I quoted it to Sergeant F., knowing him to be a Kipling worshipper, and I don't think he liked it at all . . . .

It is hopeless to make plans dependent on my movements and we must not try, for as you know we are all chattels at the disposal of the Great General Staff to be blown here or thither at a puff of their breaths . . .

In 1916, my mother went to work in a canteen in France to 'help out' with the 'war effort':

I'm glad you have had a good crowd of Belgians at your canteen. I admire the Belgians greatly; they are very brave and I don't think the French give them sufficient credit for what they have done. Now dear, at least I know where you are . . .

I wish I had you to stroke in the mud with me . . . .

The bleak cold rain is beastly. I would like a square stone house to live in . . . .

In a 'war of material' all material is very valuable: trees are not trees but cover for guns, chairs and tables are as much value to Haig Limited as they would be to Harrods Limited . . . .

I'm utterly unable to see the glamour of it, only the beastliness is very apparent . . . .

No, the dugout isn't dry now, nor is anything or anyone else in this accursed climate . . . . Nor am I dry or ever think of changing my clothes or anything else of the things I should do . . . .

My dear Mary,

We had our first smell of gas lately. There was a bad smell of chlorine, the unspeakable Huns having launched their infamous gas . . . . I was wakened by an absolutely ferocious cannonade . . . .

Do any of your Tommies sing the great song 'I Want To Go Home?' It is almost a masterpiece when it has the little tune along with it. 'I want to go home, I want to go over the sea. Oh my! I don't want to die. I want to go home.'

I must sing it to you. The tune has but a couple of bars in all and it would be very easy to improvise. It must be the sincerest war song ever written . . . .

Let me know all the things you do and how you are, also what you are going to do about your hair. And if you are going to send me a picture of it and you . . . .

I've always disliked Mme Marcievitch [sic] for the ugly face on her but I'm told she's a good woman and did well in helping the Larkin strikers. What has happened to the Abbey Theatre that you say they've gone bad? Is it that they are producing nothing only Lady Gregory's stuff now? Have they done The Playboy at all?

Yes, I left my lonely father, who had lost his Mary, who had lost his beloved daughter to a wayward Westmeath man and his soaking acres of bog and scrub, his son Noll working in the Overseas Airways in Basra. I left him alone, utterly selfish as I was, and was glad to be gone.

I was happy to forget Leixlip for a while, happy to forget my father's hopeless attempts at taming me, making me respectable. Happy to forget my lack of attempts to get to know him.

But I could not throw off this baggage of guilt towards my parents. *Daddy, it was all my fault. Daddy, I was always afraid of you.*

The Golden Spoon Is Tarnished

Yes, I had been born with a golden spoon in my mouth – well, silver, perhaps, but as I left my mother's womb it soon tarnished.

A Piscean: two steps forward and one step back. Or worse, vice versa. Cursed, I suppose, by the bad luck of my Neanderthal appearance. 'Elephant head', my mother called me – a sly laugh coming out of the side of her mouth. Once I showed her a picture of a toddler I'd found, wondering if it was me. As if I'd committed a mortal sin, she screamed at me: 'You were never as pretty as that!'

But somehow I'd scraped my way through the hills of childhood: dodging, lying, prevaricating, being non-communicative – in many ways an unattractive little brat – and here I was in Farnham working as a groom.

It was May, and the meadows were beginning to sprout; the grass was sweet and hummed with insects. The gaunt house in which I was to stay for the next three months reflected light from its windows. Square as a box, stretching out the back into a myriad of sheds and out-offices and an ancient keep, the original seat of the Maxwells – the title 'Farnham' having been bestowed on them by some English monarch a few centuries back.

Lord Farnham, ramrod-straight, military moustache, was prone to say things like 'Hff' and 'Hmm' when roused to noticing my presence. Lady Farnham, on the other hand, bushy, almost benign, with a mouth full of perfectly sculpted teeth, on meeting me took me to see the rose garden. The path wound down through a lounging lawn, past a round fountain on which sat Cupid, curled like a frog, and ended in an arbour of colour, so profuse it was blinding. But I was eager to step into the reality of my situation. They had spoken to me in the drawing room – I had already been interviewed in Dublin by the estate agent – but now, with firm, friendly tones, she informed me that I would take my meals in the servants' hall and that Annie, the lady's maid, would show me to my room.

We did not climb the main staircase, baronial with its deep carpet, but went up the back stairs, the bare boards clattering under my shoes. I followed her into the servants' quarters and into my bedroom. This was a narrow structure overlooking the yard. It was bare of furniture except for the bed and a plain wooden table, on which sat a basin and jug, and a mirror on a stand.

Saying that tea would be in half an hour, she left me there, bemused and bewildered but not unhappy.

The fair breeze coming through the open window did not quite eradicate the pervading smells of old clothes and unwashed bodies, the spoors of generations of servants who must have inhabited these quarters for centuries – although the wooden floor was scrubbed clean and the walls were a sterile white.

The soap-opera effect of the below-stairs pecking order was made clear at tea when I descended into the servants' hall. On the top rung was Tom, the butler: two-faced, efficient, sycophantically obsequious towards the lord and lady, and later to their offspring when they arrived. Then the lady's maid. The appearance of this late-middle-aged, worn person reflected her frail acceptance of her lot, and her position of trust. Lady

Farnham trusted her to wash and iron her silk nightie every day, to change her sheets every week – the best linen from Dublin – and not to steal her jewellery, her best clothes. In general, she was to be at the beck and call of this ageing aristocrat, who believed that she treated her servants well.

The meal came up to scratch. I wolfed down the cold meats and salads, the brown bread, and gulped the mahogany-coloured tea, poured by Tom from a huge tea urn. I realised immediately that I would have trouble with Tom. He was boss and no two ways about it, but my ambiguous position made it unlikely that I would accept his power. But the new girl holds her peace.

I had been told that I could use the little room set aside for the lady's maid, and after tea she took me there. It was up the back stairs and across a landing. I spent ten minutes there and never entered it again. This fussy little place, with its pretensions of gentility, its stuffed armchair, had mixed smells of old airlessness and cheap polish.

That first night I spent in my bedroom looking out at the darkening yard, I was strangely elated. Once more I had escaped parental control. I was about to earn money – ten shillings a week – for doing something that I enjoyed doing. But at the same time, a trickle of loneliness ran down my spine. I would write to Christopher, tell him I had arrived. I would not say 'I love you'. But I did not write that night. I stayed at the window till it was pitch dark and all the lights in the outhouses were extinguished. Then I lit my candle and climbed into bed.

I was in the yard at 8 AM and was met by the estate agent, who took me to the stables. There were two horses who looked to be decent sorts, and he explained that 'the Lord', as they called him, would probably be out for a ride, and I would accompany him if he wanted me to. The great bell in the yard had already clanged, and the various farmhands appeared from all corners, bleary-eyed, shuffling in to be counted and relegated to their various tasks. There was a lavatory in the corner, for the use of us outdoor workers, and useful as a smoking haunt.

My novel *Girl on a Bicycle*, although not entirely factual, has an emotional truth – which is, I suppose, its advantage. I tried to deal humorously with this strange three months, which culminated in a drastic debacle at the Cavan tennis tournament. How could I, with my traumatic background, comport myself like a normal teenager, whatever that is? Nowadays we know all about teenagers and hormones, but if I'd ever seen a hormone, I wouldn't have known what to say to it! I only knew of the list of taboos.

So we smoked and drank, when we could. We ogled boys but were terrified of sex. Sex was an ogre. And my sister, my smart beautiful sister, had gone down the road to perdition.

But now I was free. Not only from paternal anger – yes, my father had been angry since my mother died – but also from my envy of Paloma's looks and self-assurance. So those three summer months were a mixture of the idyll and a pointless search. For what? Love, I suppose. Without knowing what love was. Or that love was the greatest ogre of all.

There was Des (not his real name), the hardware merchant in Cavan town. A lonely man who went in for cross-border smuggling. Bicycle tyres and tubes and suchlike. Sometimes I kept cave for him while he sorted and rummaged in the back of the shop. The guards were on his trail but he managed to evade them. He called me his 'magazine-cover girlie' – I am not sure why – and bought me bottles of Cairns ale and brandy. When I was too drunk to ride home on my bike, he hired the hackney and drove me home. Once he put me up on the counter and ran his hand up my skirt, whereupon I jumped down and ran from the shop. Was I entering on the road to perdition? I wasn't quite sure. But it made me uneasy.

My problem was Christopher. He wrote me casual notes and I replied gushingly. He wrote in a kind of shorthand. 'Things are v. b'ing [boring] here. Maybe you cd get a job over here and we might coalesce. All my love. C.' So I thought about him night and day and, when asleep, I dreamt about my dead mother clawing at the coffin.

However, to work at something I really enjoyed was a new experience. I had a first-class mare to ride in the shows and I amused myself by playing the beautiful piano and teaching myself Italian. Lord Farnham taught me how to count sheep, a thing he did once a week, by shooing them through a gap one by one. We didn't chat on these occasions. In any case, what would I have had to say? I refused to call him 'Your Lordship', which was how his staff addressed him, and always formally said 'Yes' and 'No', or else gave him his title, 'Lord Farnham'.

He rode long-stirrup and dismounted like a cowboy, not taking his left leg out of the irons before stepping on to the ground. This amused me as I waited patiently, holding the horse's head, before trotting both his horse and mine into their stables.

Of the servants, the one I got on with best was Nelly, the kitchen maid. A buxom, smelly lass with whom I had much in common. She was the lowest rung of the ladder. Waited on the other maids and the cook. Washed the piled-up greasy saucepans, long after the others had retired. Then I would stand by her helping to dry them, making her laugh by tickling her and driving her mad with exasperation. She was the underling of the servants, I was the underling of the upstairs gentry.

She was my friend. My other most peculiar friend was Lord Farnham's cousin – the only one who didn't treat me like a menial. Because she was a little gone in the head, not quite right, off-key, she had what was called a keeper. The keeper must have had some training in mental nursing in the days when mental patients were regarded as showpieces to be watched through keyholes, to be beaten and locked in tiny cells. But the rich could afford a paid hand, a jailer, and she fell into the clichés of such people: she was rough and uncouth, and rude to me. They lived in a lovely old Georgian house, ivy-covered and surrounded by the relics of old decency: beautiful Sheraton and Chippendale furniture, silver and damask, but all dark and tarnished. Upstairs the floor sloped, water dripped down the eaves, the fire smoked, but Emily (again, not her real name) used to ask me in for tea and insist that the nurse did not accompany us. No wonder the nurse didn't like me. Her autocracy was challenged. And Emily, with her flyaway smile, would show me her treasures. She had the beauty of a little girl who couldn't grow up. But when my friendship with her leaked out, Lord Farnham told me not to visit her any more.

One of my few near sexual encounters was with the bishop's son. He lured me up into the garlic wood, ostensibly to take a spin on our bikes. On arriving at a lake, he bluntly asked me to take my knickers off. I didn't fancy this vulpine individual, who imagined himself a misunderstood intellectual. He informed me that sex was part of life that couldn't be ignored. I was not at all sure about this. When I refused to undress, he grew angry and called me a fool and a prick-tease. I jumped away and, pushing my bike through the ruts and tangled grass, at last reached the road and pedalled furiously for Farnham.

Thereafter, on a few occasions he held out a carrot of taking me to town. Once I went to the Farnham Arms and he bought us two pale dry sherries. He told me all about a play he was writing and how his mother would die if she read it. I was not impressed.

And all this time I remembered Christopher's arms and the looseness of his chest. I remembered his humorous mouth, his long brow and sexy touch. I thought his letters must mean something. And then he wrote to say he was coming to Dublin and could I meet him.

It was a very awkward moment. The grandchildren were expected. And part of my duties was to teach the young ones to ride. A few weeks earlier, I had been sent over to a village near John and Paloma's farm to fetch a pony for the youngest. That was a horrible experience. Their only income consisted of breaking in horses, mostly farm animals, for their neighbours. The way they did this was to put the animal in the shafts of a cart and gallop to the local pub. Here they tied the horse to a post, got drunk and galloped home. We went through this rigmarole and, once home, they started a row. John ended up beating the head off her with a lovely cane Emily had given me, and that I wanted to give to Paloma. It had a carved ivory head the shape of a horse and, when pulled out, could be used as a measuring stick. He beat her and beat her until the stick was in smithereens. The lovely ebony stick broken and thrown away, and my sister lying on the ground screaming. She had recently given birth to their daughter, Gail, a tiny mite of a thing, with a paid woman to look after her. I never went back to their place again. Eventually they split up, but not until she'd had her second daughter, Deirdre, a couple of years later.

But now I was not concerned with all this, although at the time it left a black hollow in my heart. I remembered that night in the pub where I had played 'In the Mood' on the pub piano, the notes falling like coins into a tin, and the awful pointlessness of the situation. But I tried to put the episode into the back of my mind as I concentrated on how to approach the Lord for a few days' leave.

After several bad starts, I managed to approach Lady Farnham and stammer out my request. 'May I have three days off before the grandchildren arrive? Please.'

That was a Thursday, and I must be back on the Monday to prepare for the onslaught: their only daughter, personal maids, governess to the children and the heir, the grandson and his timid little sister. There was a legend in the Maxwell history that the earldom always skipped a generation: sure enough, their only son had been killed in the current war.

So I took the Cavan bus on a hot day in July, with sweet-chewing children, moidered mothers in headscarves, middle-aged ladies in hats and jackets, farmers' sons on the way to catch the boat, and young lassies like myself dressed in reds and blues with stockings and pointy shoes, and calf-length skirts with a slight flare.

We went to see the latest version of *Romeo and Juliet*, with Myrna Loy, after which we had supper in a restaurant in Pembroke Street, a small place with racing prints on the walls and flowered tablecloths. Christopher got angry when the waitress said we couldn't have beer, and I quailed, holding my breath. But later we went to Doheny and Nesbit's, where we were ushered into the snug. No women allowed at the bar.

We made love in Una Moran's little house in Blackrock. A mixture of craziness and pain. Pain, because I somehow knew, before he even told me, that he thought there was no future in this, and I, who believed in a future, would return to Farnham distraught. And when I say we made love, made love in that single bed, we did not. We lay together kissing and rolling about.

'I've been fucked up by my mother,' he said. 'I just make messes on little girls' bellies.'

On the platform at Blackrock, he said, 'I hate hysterical women.'

In this unleavened state, I returned to my duties – all of which had lost their sheen. The children were knowing little brats, their governess a grim unyielding creature whom I must trundle around in a pony trap with the little girl, their maids with their wide English vowels were stupefied with terror, and, worst of all, the Honourable daughter took a real dislike to me.

So a little madness set in. I trawled Cavan for young men. The chemist's son accompanied me home one night on his bike, and I dragged him into the bushes, ran my tongue around his mouth and then ran away. I was always spied on, called a brazen hussy, 'and she on a boy's bike as well', but continued this downward spiral with lack of thought or imagination.

And then the Cavan tennis tournament. By coincidence, Iris Wellwood and her new husband were in the Farnham Arms that night. She told me how she regretted throwing me out of the Evans household and that I was the brightest kid she had ever taught, but this meant nothing to me, so steeped in terror and guilt was I – and three weeks later I knew why.

'You looked so smug when it happened to Paloma,' John Price said.

But this time I told none of my parental relations.

I left Farnham. I left my little white room. I could not stop crying. Great heart-scalding gulps tore me asunder.

'Why are you crying?' they asked.

PART FOUR

ENGLAND, 1944

I stood on the lawn at Leixlip House scuffing the newly laid turf.

'Why do you want to go to England?' my father asked.

'To help with the war effort.'

'That's a lie.'

That was a lie.

Every day in the *Irish Times* there was a square advertisement which read: 'NERVOUS SEXUAL DISORDERS TREATED'. And the name was Dr Stein, with an address in Merrion Square.

Heavy-hearted, I approached the brass-plated door. Everyone knew what he did but no one had yet proved it. And he was no doctor. He was some sort of mechanic from Austria who knew how much in demand his trade would be in Ireland. He had escaped the war and set up this lucrative business in Dublin.

'How much?' I asked.

'One hundred pounds. In advance.'

The interior of the house was like a science-fiction set. Big steel screens round a rep-covered couch with steel stirrups in which I had to insert my knees. 'Oh yes,' he said, poking, 'you are certainly pregnant.' His round Austrian faced beamed down at me. Slightly bald, with no eyebrows and a patriarchal sniff, he folded back the gear and let me off the couch.

'I don't have a hundred pounds.'

'Very well,' he said, ushering me to the door.

The sun beamed down on Merrion Square as, defeated, I continued into Nassau Street, round Trinity College to Aston Quay, where I waited for the 66 bus.

In Fitzwilliam Square, a man was recruiting Irish girls to work in a factory in Birmingham. This smarmy rat-faced individual vetted each girl as they queued up on the stairs. I was terrified he would guess my condition.

'Are you fit?'

'Of course.'

'No known disease?'

'I've had chickenpox, measles, mumps.'

'You are well now?'

'Very well.'

'You will be given a label, an address in Birmingham, and you will report at Dun Laoghaire next week.'

'Thank you, sir.'

A week later, I was on the mailboat with ten other girls, labelled like cattle. The boat zig-zagged across the Irish Sea to avoid the mines which peppered the sea bed. Early on in the war, the *Munster and Leinster* had been sunk by a mine, with the loss of all the passengers on board. The ship rolled and dived in the wintry waves and I vomited and vomited. Emptied and terrified, I arrived in Birmingham in the blackout, to be told to take a bus to a suburb called Solihull.

So here in the sooty November weather I was, yes, astray in my wits with terror. Because of the constant bombing and resultant fires, there were round watercourses everywhere. So we stumbled and cursed in the darkness as we went our various ways, myself to the central bus stop.

My wispy upper-class landlady, to whom I was introduced that night, was, I was told by the organisers, 'doing her bit' for the war effort, i.e. taking in lodgers at a low rent. I was also introduced to Nancy Colgan, with whom I would share both house and bed. Nancy, a graduate from Cork, worked in the invoice department of the factory, and I was relegated to the switchboard. The factory made parts for light aircraft; it was tucked away in the industrial centre of the city.

These are the cold facts of the desperate plight in which I found myself. Everything was grey: the city, the weather. But most of all there was the utter hopelessness, the aloneness of my situation. Not one person in this whole abominable country in whom I could confide. There was no way I could return to my beloved Dublin, never mind my house. I had to wipe my whole past away as though a great blank space lay behind me. How could I write to my friends when I couldn't tell them why I was here? In the eyes of the whole world, I was the lowest of the low. That is how I felt and that is how hundreds of Irish girls both before and after me must have felt. Because that is what society does to young women. 'Oh ho,' people can say. Times have changed now, as I write this, but the unspeakable loneliness that the young single mother bears is quite unlike any other feeling. I have written many poems for young women in this situation, but not because I felt that I ought to write them or that it was a 'good idea', a 'sympathetic subject.' No, these poems were wrenched from me – there is no other way to describe it.

I could not confide in Nancy. Not even as we lay in bed as far from each other as possible.

My enlarged breasts and swelling belly I tried to hide with corsets and loose dresses. I vomited in secret. Always hungry, always sick, we took the bus each morning, walked the mile through the wastes of the industrial estates, the mud oily and stinking rode up the backs of our stockings, the nausea as we passed Smith's crisp factory, with its smell of putrid fat, the damp, the cold, the blackout as we repeated this journey. Days, weeks dragged by. What the hell was I going to do? Where could I go?

But the human being is extraordinary. Somehow or other I taught myself to act as normally as possible. As though I was like any other girl at work in a chosen job. We played poker at break-times. I crossed the lines on the switchboard so they'd scream through the wires: 'Who's that new Irish girl on the telephone?' I mastered the Brummie language of my partner, a sweet lass who invited me once to Sunday dinner. I remember to this day the smell of roast pork as I approached her little house on the brow of a hill in a housing estate, so encased with slime and rubbish of all kinds that I had to keep swallowing my vomit as it rolled up into my mouth But the dinner was tasty, rich with gravy, and her parents loving and kind. Up till then I had thought all parents must be cruel people, bent on destroying their children. This calm English working-class household full of laughter and cats was my first glimpse into what must be normality. For a while, my natural shyness with the older generation could not open up to their hospitality. But after thinking about it – as much as I was able to think of anything other than my plight – I began to understand that the norm was comfort and warmth, and not the thorn bush of hatred from which I had escaped.

I wrote lies home to my father, and when Christmas came I lied that I had to work in the factory for extra pay. In truth, we had three days off. Nancy went home and I stayed in my lodgings.

It snowed. I wandered the streets, peering into windows filled with fairy lights and tinsel, remembered Christopher, my cousin, twenty years older than me, with his long arms, his laconic smile, his loose bones and honed cheeks. Christopher who, if he knew of my situation, might never speak to me again.

I don't know how we didn't arrange to meet. Because we still wrote to each other. And I still hoped that when at last I had had the baby adopted, we would meet and make love.

Occasionally, American GIs would try to pick us up. And on one occasion we went to a dance in a marquee and a sloppy soldier tried to kiss me. I had bought an outsize green dress for the occasion and the baby kicked the walls of my womb while I wriggled away from him, the saliva of his mouth running down my chin. Somehow I got home without being raped.

The long, dreary months passed into spring.

I told Nancy: 'I have something terrible to tell you.'

'Are you married?'

'I'm pregnant.'

I went to the social worker. And confessed.

She sent me to a farm in Surrey where I could help out till the time came. So I took myself and my load on the journey, was met at the station with a pony and trap by Pauline Buck. This woman was to be my friend and helpmeet for the next month. Her husband Frank was a baker and they had one son, Paul.

I had saved twenty-five pounds, but not a penny would they take. They even bought me cigarettes.

Yes, I had written to Christopher from my Birmingham digs, making up funny stories about my landlord and landlady. I told him about my Brummie companion on the switchboard and about the floods that happened every so often. I didn't mention the time a German plane had crashed three blocks away and how I thought it was about to hit the house, the crescendo of its whine as it descended. I didn't tell him about the sickness.

He wrote back short, crisp notes. 'Yours ever.' 'With love.' 'Dearest.'

Ingenuous Irish girls. What did we know? Fodder for the English war. Without qualifications. One by one we melted into this foreign atmosphere. Got to like it, even, the freedom, the anonymity. But for me that was later, when it was all over. My secret war. The war between my heart and my body.

Going to work in the dark. Stumbling home in the dark. Suddenly the horror had stopped.

Here I was in sunny May, feeding the Bucks' pigs, driving the pony trap, playing their piano. It was not amazing, somehow, to be pregnant. I was not the only sinner in the world. Other girls got pregnant outside marriage. And the planet didn't stop revolving.

The baby was three weeks overdue. It was late May. An uneasy time. Tanks everywhere. The war was hotting up. Britain was preparing for an invasion. Even amongst the bluebells where I walked with Paul – a rounded fellow in his fifteenth year – anxiety hung in the air. A pilot in a wheelchair visited. Half his face was gone, built up with plastic surgery, a mound of dough on the right where his eye should have been. A relation of Pauline's. The baby knocked and plummeted as I tried not to stare at his broken features. With loops of speech, he talked to his cousin. Then he was taken back to the small cotttage hospital where he was being treated. The same hospital where the next day I would go to have my child.

In the stratosphere of my mind, I clung on to that nebulous time when I would no longer be anchored by my load. When I'd walk free again.

In the hospital that night, we heard the air-raid siren. Long and relentless, it whined while I toiled the corridors. I prayed that the bombs would not hit us till my child was born. I must feel that freedom before I died. I cowered over each contraction. White faces stared till the all-clear went.

I was two days in labour. If I had longed for it all to be over in Birmingham, I longed more in this hygienic building.

A nine-pound baby was delivered of me. I called him Sean. I brought him home to the Bucks.

I was thin. Food tasted normal. There was a lightness in me.
I had wings on which I could soar. The sky brightened, the grass
grew greener. I played the piano, tacked up the pony and drove
to the station to meet Christopher.

'You must tell him,' Pauline Buck had said to me.

'I cannot.'

'He will understand.'

So I had written. And he was coming to see me.

Sean lay in his cot, a dark angry infant. Every four hours I
held him in my arms, the bottle to his lips.

I tried to tell myself I loved him.

I was a monster in the eyes of other mothers.

In the drawing room that afternoon, we played a duet: one
of Bach's two-part inventions in F major. He the bass, I the
treble.

'I will arrange the adoption.'

I pretended to care.

'It's all your fault,' I said.

He said 'I know. But you must tell the real father.'

The man with the head like the Caesars in my Latin book?
Tell him about the infant, Sean?

'Write to him now. I'll dictate.'

I didn't write. He must never know.

And I was in the terrible pain of love. Hopeless. Ever since
we had looked for tennis balls in the shrubbery, all the time I
worked in Farnham, all the time I was pregnant in Birmingham.
I was in love with him while I paced the corridors of the hospital and I was in love with him as we sat in the Bucks' sitting
room and played a Bach duet. And I was in love with him as we
discussed the bureaucratic web of the adoption laws.

The dusk fell that sunny afternoon, and he told me he
thought there was a woman with whom he could live. She lived
under the horror of German Vls. The doodlebugs. 'A woman.'

He said it with a laconic half-smile. I nodded. A woman. Not me. A woman.

He arranged the papers. A local family was located. A well-got homestead. There Sean would lie in his pram under the waving summer leaves. He would grow and prosper. He would giggle and smile at his mother and father. They would all drive to the seaside. Brighton. Bournemouth. They would change his name from Sean to Charles.

The year of my life I had lost would take many more years to replace.

PART FIVE

LONDON

I went to London.

My mother's brother, Maurice Collis, who lived in Maidenhead, gave me house room. His wife, Eleanor, a literary comic, was the best of company. Originally from Greystones, she had married Maurice after he'd divorced his first wife. There were grown-up sons from the first marriage, mysteriously away, and from this alliance there was a daughter, Louise, at university in Reading, and a young boy, His Majesty the Baby.

Maurice, fussy with his hands, full of obliquities, was then the art critic of the *Observer*. He took me to galleries and exhibitions, taught me how to look at paintings. He introduced me to Topolski, a painter and a rogue who called me '*La plus jolie niece a Londres*'. It was true: in some magic way my looks had suddenly improved. This was no doubt due to post-puerperal hormone changes. (Years later, I was discovered to have an overactive pituitary gland, which accounts for the large size of my head.)

Apart from Topolski, we met other painters. In particular I remember Mervyn Peake. The Peakes lounged on leopard-skin rugs and drank mint tea. Meanwhile I worked in the Chinese embassy as secretary to the military attaché. It was easy for us Irish, if we had a modicum of education, to get such a high-sounding job. Firms and organisations were desperate for secretaries as ninety percent of the single English girls had been called into the Land Army or sundry military jobs. My stint in the lavatory at Miss Galway's stood to me. I took the train every night to Maidenhead.

The V1s were peppering London, inducing in me at times the cold sweat of panic. I could not face the air-raid shelters: since my brother had tried so often to smother me under a pillow, I had a horror of being buried alive. So I'd strain to listen to them as they flew up the Thames, and when the engine went off I'd count to four, waiting for the explosion. It was like when, as a child, I had counted to four after the lightning flash till the thunder came. But with all this imagined rise in the world of culture, I was still the uneducated ingénue, pretending I knew more than I did.

In spite of all this, I decided to move into the city. Much as I liked my uncle and aunt, the journey up and down was a curse. Besides, I needed more freedom. To trawl London for men, to find a respite from my intolerable ache for Christopher. But digs were hard to find. In the first one, the landlady threw me out because, the cold being intense, I'd borrowed an army coat to put over my bed.

'We'll 'ave no soldiers 'ere!' she screamed. When I tried to explain that the coat was without a soldier in it, she wouldn't listen and forthwith threw me, and my belongings, on to the street.

The second one, in Paddington, turned out to be a whorehouse, where the fleas hopped around like hayseed and the 'girls' sat gossiping till the madame gave them a job. When a boyfriend visited me, the madame asked him was he booked in. 'Ten shillings,' she said, 'or out you go.' In another one, I was thrown out for cooking a stew which 'stank the whole house', the landlady said. I called a cab once more, books and clothes thrown in the back. 'That 'er?' the taxi driver asked as the gorgon waved from the steps.

I had two books I carried around with me: *A Portrait of the Artist* by Joyce and the Yeats poetry anthology I had won at school. For the remainder of my education, I relied on the Paddington Lending Library. Here I trawled through the nineteenth-century French and English and Russian classics, discovered that Flann O'Brien was the same person as Myles na gCopaleen, read *At Swim-Two-Birds* and, in spite of the bombs and my myriad landladies, was deliriously happy.

I was earning five pounds a week: a phenomenal sum. I swanned around in high-heeled shoes and sexy outfits and gradually, one way and another, accumulated a set of boyfriends who phoned me at the embassy for meals and surreptitious kisses. But since my experience with the Roman-profiled cowboy, I made sure that no hand would go near my pubis. And certainly no penis.

Through my godmother, Sally Wilkinson, who now lived in London, and her son, a student at Paddington Hospital, I met a selection of monumentally boring medical students. Jolly, jolly fellows who told dirty jokes and had no interest whatsoever in literature.

I had finally found a pleasant room in Bayswater, in a house owned by an Irish couple, for five shillings a week. This left me plenty of money to spend on outrageous clothes. And in what spare time I had, I wrote short stories – as like James Joyce's as possible – which were all returned from the magazines. Nothing daunted, I embarked on a novel and filled exercise books with my clumsy writing. But alas, this also went to the wastebasket.

I discovered Tolstoy and Dostoevsky, Gogol and Turgenev. I was in thrall to them.

Nancy and I often went to the Albert Hall for a concert. Sometimes the Hallé Orchestra was there, and we heard some fabulous symphonies. On another occasion I remember being stunned by Yehudi Menuhin's playing of Beethoven's violin concerto in the Wigmore Hall.

But the Germans were busy with a last-minute throw of the dice. There were rumours of rocket bombs: missiles that would come without warning and destroy half of London.

One day I was acting the maggot with a minor embassy official when we heard a shattering explosion. No sirens. No warning.

'It must be a gas-mains explosion,' he said.

We both stared out the window, not looking at each other.

'Yes, it must,' I said, and went back to work.

It had been the first V2 that we had heard that day. Silently they descended, with a rocket-head that could cause damage over an area of several square miles. They were as terrifying as the VIs. You could not strain to listen for them and count, as you could for the V1s, and just lay imagining them quietly hurtling through the sky, aiming directly at your house.

London shifted in fear. People went back to live in the Underground. Going to work meant tripping over sleeping bodies under blankets, with their thermos flasks and sandwiches strewn around them. Still we stayed in our digs: dying immediately seemed preferable to being buried alive.

Then, becoming ambitious, Nancy and I moved into a smarter house. An apartment on Leinster Road. Old Victorian elegance, large windows, a veranda, a wide mantelshelf on which cavorted marble cupids. It was the beautiful May weather of 1945, and beneath our window the plane trees, with their delicate new leaves, bordered the street as if, in spite of man's crass stupidity, all was perfect with the world.

The apartment was bigger than our previous ten-foot-by-four-foot bedsits but we were still confined to one room and two beds. There was a gas ring, and a bathroom and lavatory on the landing was for the use of all the tenants.

There was an airy abandon about the place that suited us. Polish refugees combed the balconies for customers for black-market goods, chiefly silk stockings. They'd wave the stockings in front of our window in an effort to lure us out. They were lonely, downtrodden and homesick. Worse than the Irish. Nancy went out with one once, but she said he was shabby and useless.

And it was here that we were bombed out.

The accelerating whine of the V2 alerted us a split second before the explosion. Simultaneously our beds drifted across the floor, plates of ceiling crashed on us, the house shifted, plaster settled, and gradually, gradually, everything seemed to slow down. Simultaneously we burrowed through the crumbling mortar, gagging on its acrid smell. We gazed at each other, our teeth blackened, our faces masked with dust. The street was full of noise, people yelling, sirens wailing, but inside all had become eerily quiet, as if the house itself had done its best and could do no more. We laughed hysterically, our faces cracking. We laughed at being alive, at the marble Cupids cavorting in the debris, heads and limbs disjointed, broken.

'I can't find my sandals.'

'Where's my coat?'

The staircase had tumbled into the basement. A decapitated neighbour hung from his legs, which were trapped by a beam.

We could just see across the road through the settling dust. A block of flats appeared to have been knifed in half.

Wallpaper fluttered in the breeze. A toilet bowl bulged into the air. Bedsteads poked through holes. There was terrible screaming somewhere.

We looked at each other, two beings quite unharmed. How was this? Some survived and others didn't: the trick of the fall-out from the bomb. At the time we took our luck for granted, and it was not until much later that we became aware of how shocked we had been. We simply knew that we had to get out of the house as quickly as possible.

Red Cross workers called up for survivors. 'Answer,' I said to Nancy. 'No, you,' she whispered. I called 'Hi', my voice muffled by my dust-clogged mouth. I tried to spit, and called again.

'Here. First floor.' A helmet appeared through a broken window, and the blackened face of the Red Cross worker followed. Gingerly we picked our way over the rubble, the ceiling plaster, the broken furniture, and one by one he lowered us to the ground.

The workers continued to search for bodies. Once in a while there was a cry as a mutilated corpse was pulled out. The dead were laid in rows. The efficiency of the Red Cross told of long experience. We were given blankets and cups of tea from a canteen in a van. There were others alive. We recognised one of the Poles from next door, his face grey, his lips shaking. And a strange old woman who often passed us without speaking was sitting on a folding stool while she ringed her fingers round her cup, as though she were at a picnic.

It was about 9 AM by the time the ambulances had collected all the people who were still alive. The corpses would be sorted later. They had to be identified if possible.

We were told to stand well away from our building. Yet in spite of the damage, the walls still stood more firmly than those of the block of flats beyond.

Finally we arrived at a depot, where clothes were handed out. We returned to the Irish family without a stitch of our own, like two circus clowns.

All my pretty clothes, my books, my folders of stories were buried forever. And Nancy, who was more phlegmatic than me, just shrugged off her losses. 'I suppose we're alive,' she said.

The Chinese embassy had moved, and I was made redundant. But with my spurious experience I applied to the Iranian embassy – and was taken on as second secretary to the ambassador.

My immediate superior was a real cow of a woman. When the boss sent for me, she'd come over to my desk and deliberately jostle me so that my notes got scattered. For the first time

I encountered real resentment from a fellow worker. Then the press attaché took a fancy to me and started taking me out to expensive restaurants and to the races. I quoted poetry to him to put him off, but this only made him more obsessed. Finally the inevitable happened. I agreed to go to his apartment: fair game, the fool I was. But before he had a chance to drag me into bed, I snatched my coat and ran out the door. The following morning I was given the sack, having been politely told that I was too young for the job.

I'd had similar experiences in the Chinese embassy, but each time I'd extricated myself before things got too bad. No such thing as 'sexual harassment' in those days. You just had to put up with it – and do a runner, if necessary.

I was already having great difficulty in sleeping since the bombing. As soon as I lay down, my body stiffened. I'd clutch the pillow, straining to hear enemy planes or screaming missiles. To this day, in fact, whenever a plane flies overhead I automatically duck.

Suddenly the war ended. It was extraordinary. London's streets filled up with people. The lights went on. Nancy and I squeezed along with the crowds, jubilant. No more bombs, Vls or V2s. Germany had been defeated.

By the end of July, it seemed the obvious thing to take the mailboat home for a break. I extracted some of my savings and set off from Euston Station. At the ferry, jammed to capacity, we queued for hours, shoving like cattle to get aboard. This was my first time to go home since I had left that dark day in my pregnant state, and it was with some misgivings that I faced the journey.

How would my father behave towards me? Of course he had written to me often, as I to him, but his letters were forbidding notes, and if I didn't answer quickly I dreaded his next letter.

Sometimes, in fact, it took me days to open the envelope and I wished that I could disappear forever.

But I had to go back. Ireland was under my skin, Leixlip was my alma mater. There I had learnt how to survive. And as the boat zigzagged, the decks became awash with vomit, which ran in rivulets between the seats. Accordions played, and we sang the come-all-yes and drank bottles of stout, which was served from a hatch to starboard.

We hollered out the songs – 'Galway Bay', 'It's Moonlight in Mayo', 'I'm a Rambler, I'm a Gambler and a Long Way from Home . . . ' – and the ship ploughed on through the Irish Sea.

What had I achieved during those months in London? A veneer of confidence, perhaps. A desultory education from the world's literature. A lost love, which still clutched the shreds of my heartstrings, but which I had stifled with the love of my anonymous life and its freedom.

So without warning my father, I arrived at Leixlip House in the early morning. It was the beginning of August 1945.

As I ran into my father's study, I suddenly realised he was not alone. He was with a man with pop eyes and a wild smile. The man scrutinised me as my father interjected with: 'You didn't tell me you were coming.'

At once I was made feel guilty. I stammered something: 'I didn't. . . . Sorry.'

'I'm Barney Heron,' the stranger said. 'I've taken over the factory.'

I knew nothing about this, but the very presence of this man caused a shiver of anticipation to run through me.

'I'm Leland Hone,' I said, like some sort of idiot.

'I know,' he said, and laughed deeply.

My wits astray, I muttered that I'd better unpack, and hurried out.

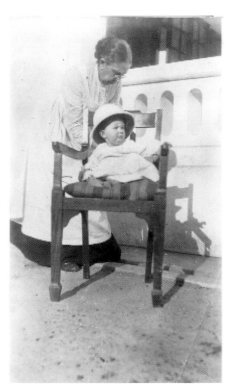

Leland and Ayah in India

Paloma in India

Leland's second birthday

'Along came a spider . . . '
Leland, 1920s

Alexandra School, Lower Fifth, 1937
Back row, left to right: Joan Eccles, Margaret Hartished, Kitsy Mitchel, Daphne
    Greening, Leland Hone, Ethel Johnson
Middle row: Joan McKeever, Maureen Neill-Watson, Sheila Kelly, Muriel Bell
Front Row: Oona Lewis, Katherine Orr, Pat McKegnee, Ethel Devlin, Joyce Dunlo
    Pat Clarke, Moira Gall

Kilquhanity House School, where the author taught in the late 1940s

With Mick Bardwell and the twins, Billy and Anna, Kilkenny, 1949

Leland, 1962

English novelist and poet Sir Kingsley Amis (1922–95) with his wife Hillary (the author's former sister-in-law) and children Philip, Sally and (right) Martin, the future novelist and journalist, outside their house in Swansea, 18 June 1956

(Photo by Daniel Farson/Hulton Archive/Getty Images)

Opposite page, top: Scottish painters Robert Colquhoun (1914–62) and Robert MacBryde (1913–66) in the studio they shared in Kensington, London, *c.* 1945
(Photo by Felix Man/Hulton Archive/Getty Images)

Opposite page, bottom: Young men at the Soho bar and nightclub La Caverne, 16 July 1955

(Photo by Joseph McKeown/Picture Post/Hulton Archive/Getty Images)

A busy night in the York Minster
pub in Dean Street, Soho, London,
22 October 1955

(Photo by Frank Pocklington/Picture
Post/Hulton Archive/Getty Images)

Author Anthony Burgess
with his books.

(Photo by Marvin Lichtner/Time Life
Pictures/Getty Images)

Patrick Kavanagh, Katherine Moloney and wedding guests, 1977
(Image courtesy of the National Library of Ireland)

Paddy O'Brien in Grogan's

In Hatch Place, Dublin, 1970s

Poster from Co-op Books announcing the publication of the author's novel *Girl on a Bicycle* (1977)

NEW IRISH FICTION from Co~oP Books

GIRL ON A BICYCLE

BY LELAND BARDWELL

Julie de Vraie fights against her Protestant background, her Catholic country and ultimately herself. A novel of wit and candour set in Ireland of the '40's, by one of our foremost women poets.

Paperback £1.50

NOW RE-ISSUED:

THE IKON MAKER

a novel by

DESMOND HOGAN

'Anyone interested in contemporary Irish fiction should read this book.'
—TOM MACINTYRE, BOOKS IRELAND

Paperback £1.25

NOW RE-ISSUED:

NIGHT IN TUNISIA

and other stories by

NEIL JORDAN

'NIGHT IN TUNISIA...is one of the most remarkable stories that I have read in Irish storytelling since, or indeed before Joyce.'
—SEAN O'FAOLAIN R.T.E.

Paperback £1.25

ORDER FROM:
Irish Writers'Co-operative,
4 Victoria Road,
Clontarf,
Dublin 3

Michael Hartnett at Paddy O'Brien's funeral near Slane

Patrick Kavanagh and Anthony Cronin seated in carriage outside Davy Byrne's pub,
Bloomsday 1954, Duke Street, Dublin

Opposite page, top: In Hatch Place, Dublin, 1970s

Opposite page, bottom: Anthony Cronin, John Ryan and Flann O'Brien at architect
Michael Scott's house, Bloomsday 1954, Sandycove, Dublin

With Dermot Seymour (far left) and Sunday guests in Cloonagh, County Sligo

Katherine Kavanagh and John Jordan, after Kavanagh's funeral

Leland outside Farnham House, on tour after publication of *Mother to a Stranger* (2002)

John Jordan addressing the crowd at the annual St Patrick's Day commemoration for Patrick Kavanagh, 1970s

Macdara Woods (front) and John McCarter share a joke with photographer Letty Mooring outside McDaid's pub in the 1960s, as Patrick Kavanagh walks away.

The author's daughter Jacky at an exhibition in Dublin, 1960s

The author's sons Ed, John (front) and Nick, at St Patrick's Secondary School in Dublin, 1970s

In Cloonagh, County Sligo, 2005

In my old room, I threw my case on the bed and looked out of the window. Why were my legs wobbling? What was going on?

My father had given up the unequal task of continuing to run the factory against all odds. So Barney had taken over the lodge and was intending to construct a kiln in order to dry the native timber.

It was a hitherto unheard-of situation because it turned out that he was living with a married woman. Leixlip must be agog. He had already been married, and his wife was somewhere – 'a tiger woman', he told me later – and this new partner was called Rosemary.

Yes, he wanted for nothing when it came to sexual villainy. Here was I in my smart London clothes, a ball of wild energy, and there was he, ready to pounce.

The horse show was on, and we all set off to see the finery. Although for some reason or other Rosemary did not accompany us.

On the way home that hot August day, just after leaving Chapelizod, he stopped the bus, pulling me after him. Hotfoot, we plunged down a side road and into a field. In half a minute my clothes were scattered in the cowslips and he was fucking me blind. At some point he assured me he wouldn't make me pregnant. And as casual as bedamned, he jumped away, stood up, buttoned up his flies and helped me to my feet.

What was I supposed to do now, ingénue that I was, and once more in thrall to a man some twenty years older than I was?

He drove an old Ford 8 on paraffin oil. At any moment he'd give me the nod and we'd be off into the woods or across the fields.

'Bring the dog' – a white bull terrier – 'and he'll keep watch for footsteps.'

'I must go back to London.'

'Why?'

'I mustn't lose my work permit.' (Since the war with Japan was still raging, the Control of Engagements Order was still in force, and we Irish had to sign at the nearest police station once a month in order to be allowed to continue working.)

'I like your shoulders. The sexiest part of you. You're the sexiest person on the Captain's Hill.'

'That wouldn't be hard.'

He growled humorously and licked the inside of my mouth.

'So you stole a woman from her husband?'

'The eternal yes.'

'And now she's pregnant.'

'You've noticed.'

With a chin like asphalt, he scoured my body – my thighs, my breasts – and after each fuck I lay like a stone, wondering . . . what?

I tried to interest myself in the family goings-on. Visited my Aunt Olive. Attempted to paint my room, which was grimy and damp. But with a glimpse of his jacket, I threw down my brush and ran through the trees.

'I am really going tomorrow.'

He started up the Ford and it coughed and spluttered up to the Moor of Meath.

He pushed me into a furze bush.

'Jesus, Barney, the thorns.'

'You're a bitch. Stay.'

'I fucking can't. You know. And what about Rosemary?'

'She's a bitch, too. But I happen to love her.'

The next day, without warning, I set off to Dun Laoghaire and, standing astern, I watched the receding Irish coast – Howth Head, Bray Head – till they dipped over the horizon.

I may have cried, but I don't think so. 'Amen,' I said.

(Barney Heron is portrayed as Bernard in *Girl on a Bicycle*, juxtaposed from Leixlip to County Cavan, very much as he was:

sophisticated, travelled, villainous – and heinously attractive.)

In August that year, the Americans bombed Hiroshima and then Nagasaki, and the Japanese capitulated. We had no idea then what a terrible act this was. News dribbled in about ferocious slaughter and much worse, but our initial reaction was one of colossal relief. The whole war at last was over. The skies over London were clear. Now maybe I could lie in bed without that coil of anxiety inside me.

So I went back to my digs with the Irish couple, their soaking children and extraordinary friendship. I found a job (much lack of prestige) in an office that made office equipment. And I spent all day typing out invoices and yawning. I picked up on boring old associations and the days darkened.

One November day I got a phone call from Barney. He'd be over in a week. I had started on another novel, as bad as the first, filling up my exercise books with illegible scrawl. I threw the book out of the window and went to Euston to meet him.

I'd spent several hours in front of the mirror changing my dresses. I finally settled on a black number with a white lace collar, terribly demur! I stood on the platform waiting for the Irish mail. Not to mention 'male'.

We got drunk. We got drunk five days in a row. And he returned to Ireland.

I watched the Irish mail depart: Paddies with their brown suitcases, girls escaping from the grime of gap-toothed masonry that London had become. He smiled loosely from the window of his carriage.

'Cheerio, Barney,' I said.

Although now the war was over I still suffered from delayed shock. I had hoped that I would be able to cope with it – in Ireland it had seemed all right – but every time a plane flew over I'd duck, and then strain to listen till it was out of earshot. But I admitted this to no one. I don't think Nancy had the same terror: she had gone to the Orkneys on a job, so I had no one with whom to compare notes. And, as I said, to this day I have an uneasy feeling when I hear an aeroplane or a helicopter over-head.

And now, at twenty-two, I had been rightly fucked up by two men, had an illegitimate child, had saved a hundred pounds, and was busy writing stories, à la Joyce, that no one wanted to pub-lish.

Then Christopher rang. He was free from his job in Intelligence and now intended to go back to Cambridge and study medicine with a view to becoming a psychiatrist. 'An old man of forty-five,' he said. 'And why not?' Would I come down?

Once more in his bed. Trapped like a fly in a web.

Forget the books. Get out and play a bit of tennis.

The week before, I'd answered an ad in the *New Statesman* for a job in Kilquhanity School, in Scotland.

'Oh yes. A. S. Neill and all that.' Christopher laughed down at me in his loose-limbed way as he told me about Summerhill, and vaguely outlined the methods of Free Schooling. That the children only went to lessons when it pleased them. And that Kilquhanity House was an offshoot of the system.

'I'm trying to write a novel.' He was warm in the single bed. 'And your woman friend?'

'Oh yes.'

I got grumpy. 'I'm not just a plaything.'

He looked over to me with his usual urbanity.

My wits astray again, I returned to Paddington. There had been a phone call from John Aitkenhead, the founder of the school, and its headteacher, for me to come immediately. I took the train back to Cambridge.

Christopher received me cordially. The last thing I wanted was a cordial reception. I wanted to tell him about Barney Heron and travels in the meadows that smelled of cowslips and mown hay. I wanted to tell him so many things. I wanted to tell him I loved him and wanted to live with him for the rest of my life. And that I'd gladly play tennis forever if he'd let me stay.

I took the train back to London.

Some time later, he asked me why I had come back. Unable to tell him, I shrugged my shoulders to save my pride from its final disintegration.

PART SIX
KILQUHANITY HOUSE

I married Michael Bardwell in Dumfries, the birthplace of Robert Burns. I wanted so badly to get drunk with John and Morag Aitkenhead, but Michael was recovering from peritonitis so we sat around playing the gramophone, sharing half a bottle of whiskey between the four of us.

I had joined a crew of derelicts and ne'er-do-wells. Willingly. I had thrown away my London gear, put on a kaftan and long strings of beads and proceeded to take part in what was a precursor to hippie-dom.

In fact the derelicts were simply underfed and traumatised by their recent experiences during the war. Most of them had been conscientious objectors and had been subjected to the most advanced forms of humiliation and cruelty. Some had spent the war years in jail and others had been used as guinea pigs for experiments in scurvy and suchlike. They told of having to stand in cold water for hours at a time while they were injected with many diseases, including the common cold. The result was that although they were still young, most of them had aged expressions and few had any teeth left.

Michael also had been a CO, as they were called, but he had been represented by the Quakers at his tribunal and, although he had to leave Cambridge, where he was studying English, he had spent his war years working as an orderly in a hospital. This was known as 'essential' work. These people, even though they were unqualified to look after children, had drifted to Kilquhanity to find a niche for themselves and their traumatised minds.

The headmaster, John Aitkenhead, a qualified teacher with a Masters in Education from Glasgow, had fallen foul of the conventional system and become a follower of A. S. Neill, the pioneering educationalist. Having asked Neill whether he should start a school of his own, and being told 'No', he did so anyway. He acquired an unoccupied house near Castle Douglas in Kirkcudbright and, with little money but a store of enthusiasm, started his school in the beautiful setting of the Lowlands.

This was a few years before the war began. Times were hard. With one other qualified teacher, and a couple of helpers, pupils trickled in. Fees were minimal, and the local authorities were not impressed with this bare, uncarpeted building, where rusty water issued from the taps. But when the war came, things brightened up for John. Rich parents began removing their children from boarding schools in the south of England and sending them to the safety of the Scottish countryside. Small improvements could be made. But of course, with the end of the war these snobbish people reinstated their offspring in their posh schools, and once more John was left with the detritus sent there from orphanages and reform schools, or the children of penniless artists and writers, who believed in the system of free education. These people usually ended up working for nothing in the school in order to pay their children's fees. One of these people was Valda Grieve, the wife of the poet Hugh McDiarmid. When I arrived, she was working in the kitchen to pay the fees for her son, Michael.

Valda was a feisty redhead awash with stories about her wayward husband. They had lived on the Orkneys, and she told how, in order to prevent him leaving, she had locked him in the house and hidden all his clothes. And how he had managed to escape out the window and run naked to a neighbour, where clothes – and a boat – were procured.

He had a great way with women. On one occasion, after he had disappeared, she followed him to London and visited a prostitute, a friend of both of them. While the woman was entertaining a client, she was in the other bed, whereupon the client turned to her, asking her if she was all right or if she needed a go! Anyway, she found his address, in a London suburb. On her arrival at the house, the door was opened by a lady, much dyed and powdered. 'Who are you?' Valda asked. 'Mrs Grieve,' the other replied, to which Valda returned: 'So am I!'

Anyway, when I arrived at the school, all John could afford to pay us was ten shillings a week. To this was added food and board, and shoe mending.

Undeterred by my drop in salary, I was quite quickly seduced by the free atmosphere and the warm personalities of John and his wife, Morag. I was undeterred also by the angry letters from home. Why had I given up my good salaried jobs, where I might have got somewhere? 'Irresponsible' was the word used to describe me!

Yes, at Kilquhanity it was as if I had found a family which I had never had. On the other hand, I was hopeless with children. I couldn't keep order. I couldn't teach them anything. My first duties were to look after and house-mother five delinquent ten-year-olds. Even getting them to bed was a nightmare. They'd tear the bedroom asunder, with bedclothes – and sometimes beds – being fired out of the window. When I took them for walks, they climbed up the trees like monkeys and pissed on my head. Or when I took them swimming in the burn, they tore off their clothes and ran around naked, prompting strait-laced neighbouring Presbyterians to lodge a complaint to the local authority. This did not endear me to the Aitkenheads.

The only thing I was good at was scrubbing pots and pans while Mick Bardwell did the cooking. We ate mounds of lentils and split peas, stovies (a dish of potatoes, carrots and mutton fat), and porridge made from pinhead oatmeal, and tried to convince ourselves that we were pioneers.

The reform-school kids had endearing criminal characteristics. They rummaged in your cupboards, stole any money they could find, and went off to Dumfries or Castle Douglas, returning with armfuls of toys of all kinds – model-aeroplane kits and the like – which they distributed amongst the less enterprising. I remember one, Ian, an orphan who had been mercilessly beaten. He believed he had royal parentage, and adopted a stance like a latter-day Fagin. At thirteen, he held them all in thrall.

However, it was not all chaos. With some, the system worked. Lessons were not compulsory, but so strong was John's personality that his classes were popular enough to entice even the most diligent villain.

John was not just a genial father figure. His rare gift for teaching made him head and shoulders above the average *dominie*. He also did most of the farm work, milking the cows, feeding the hens and digging the garden. His energy was phenomenal.

With my low success rate in the teaching stakes, I soon discovered the one creative thing I could do with a modicum of authority. Teach musical appreciation and, to the more gifted, music.

One fellow, who was around ten when I met him, had a superb ear and could do anything on the tin whistle. He had reading problems, however, and not even John could get him over that initial hump. I decided to attempt to teach him the notes on the piano. In half a day, he had mastered the treble and bass clef, and thereafter we often played duets – to the joy of listeners. The breakthrough in music having reduced his anxieties, in a very short time he learnt to read, and he went on to be quite a scholar.

On the whole, the children were happy there. And when it came time for them to leave, many of them begged to be allowed to stay on to work there. Valda's son, Michael, started working in the kitchen when he was eighteen. Thrown out on the world after Kilquhanity, it was hard for them to adapt. But they weren't all dropouts: Graham McLachlan, one of Michael's peers, went to Edinburgh University, but sadly died before he graduated. He was one of many who had been mercilessly punished by his father.

Yes, they came and went, as did the teachers and helpers. Some, very tortured by their past, drifted off after a few months. One woman, the wife of an assistant teacher, lay in bed all day in the depths of depression. She could not eat in public, so when everyone was in bed, she'd creep down to the kitchen and eat out of the cupboard. Another, John, roamed in and out of bedrooms at night, turning on taps in the bathroom, banging his forehead with his fist and hinting at terrible wartime experiences. He had been in the army, but nobody knew what had really happened to him: he was unable to finish a sentence, which would trail off into darkness. His pleas for attention were never assuaged. Eventually, he put all his belongings into cornflake packages and was carted off to Dumfries mental institution. When some of us decided to visit him, he didn't recognise us. His mind shone through vacant eyes: he paced the waiting room, muttering at the windows and doors till a white-coated nurse led him back to his quarters.

Communal farms and educational establishments were not new. As is known, Middleton Murray had started one in the twenties with followers like D. H. Lawrence. Believers in love and co-operation. Believers in peace and goodwill. As I said, my family was horrified at my decision to leave my 'good' jobs in London in order to don sandals and rags in pursuit of a 'cause.' We were no pretty people like the later hippies, however. We lived rough and worked hard. We ran around, passing each other in corridors, like nurses in the emergency ward. We could never catch up with the chores, and our efforts to please our mentor, John, often went unnoticed. It was not surprising that we leant on each other – dropouts always cling together – and that unsuitable relationships were formed *faute de mieux*.

I got a letter from my father sometime around then. He said that he planned to get married and would sell Leixlip House. My brother, back home and married, would get the money from the sale and build himself a house with the proceeds. On the one hand, I was delighted. I had always dreaded that I'd end up living with my father when he got too old to live by himself. On the other, I worried about the loss of all my juvenilia – which Noll eventually burnt – and my myriad treasures. Most of all, though, I worried about losing my room – but not enough to drop my work and go home to give a hand with the move. I was caught up with my new experience of a 'family' and it was not until some years later that I fully realised what the loss of my room meant. Never again would there be a place for me to touch down. After my father's wedding, and his move to his future wife's house, it was like being in an aeroplane that had no runway to land on, with no choice but to fly round and round forever.

Illness at Kilquhanity was not condoned. Once, running a temperature of 103, as I lay in bed hallucinating, I was told that there was nothing wrong with me. And it was cold, always cold. Scoops of freezing air ran up and down the uncarpeted stairs, crept under the bedroom doors. So at length, Michael Bardwell and I crept into bed together.

We shared a love of classical music, and most of our spare time was spent lying on the floor, winding up the old gramophone and playing Bach or Beethoven, or sundry seventy-eights. Michael was a year younger than me, tall, good-looking in a conventional way, and a slow mover who held his forehead before making a decision. But he was not without a sense of humour.

Soon it evolved that he wanted to marry me, I'm not sure why. Our relationship was workaday. No wild passion, no aching highs and lows. I agreed, and again I am not sure why. But in those days, women had two choices: marriage or degrading spinsterhood. The latter meant plain old age, do-gooding and sacrifice, the former a slot in conventional society, while (I imagined!) maintaining one's own individuality.

The chief reason I accepted was perhaps the fact that I felt that I had lost Christopher once and for all. So I slipped into the situation, telling myself – and my father and aunt – that I loved him.

They were angry. They wanted me to come home and get married in a church, but Mick was anti-religion of any kind and, like a dog on a string, I went along with his ideas. Although terrified still of the trappings of the Protestant religion, I was more afraid of my parent's anger. I wanted to go home, to make a last attempt at bridging the gap. But I buried the dilemma in my mind, pretending that I was strong enough to defeat my misgivings.

The date was fixed. But during the fierce snows of '47, when the whole of Scotland (and Ireland) lay down under a stretched white canvas, Mick got violently ill. Somehow the doctor got through, and he diagnosed a burst appendix, and peritonitis. We postponed the wedding.

When he was back in school recuperating, I realised my mistake. How could I tell him? How could I hurt him when he was still a sick man?

A month later, John, Morag, Mick and I set off in a bus to Dumfries. I wore a pale-green suit, and a white shirt and a white hat. I do not remember what the others wore. There were no wedding photographs, no drunken celebrations. We returned to Kilquhanity, played Bach on the gramophone, shared the already-mentioned bottle of whiskey and went to bed.

175

PART SEVEN

IRELAND

We packed our bags and came to Ireland.

During that year in Kilquhanity, I had not done much writing. I had staged a play by Flann O'Brien with the senior boys. Much hilarity. I had painted a lot. I was much taken by the rugged landscape of the Lowlands, which in parts is not unlike the west of Ireland. And in any spare time I had, I'd be off with my poster paints and paper, putting down my impression of the terrain. The overlying colours of that landscape are blues of various hues. A harsh, unyielding world of small farms dragging a living out of the land. I got caught up with the stones and would spend hours on one wall. All this sounds very amateurish now and, of course, what you might call Impressionist. With great pleasure and pride, I gave a painting to my Aunt Olive, who burst out laughing. 'It doesn't look like anything.'

After this, Impressionism took a back seat. I got into Dublin scenes, stick-like Lowry-esque figures. Children swinging on lampposts and suchlike. The pictures began to tell stories. (I suppose I've always been a storyteller.) But I had no talent really, and couldn't draw for the life of me. I did, however, take much pleasure in these excursions into the visual arts.

Michael was the writer now. His mother doted on him and had kept all his scribblings since he was a wain. He was quite a good cartoonist and used to write quirky anecdotes, which he illustrated himself. But now we must find a cottage, fit for a real writer. Yes, he would write a novel, and I'd do something, I wasn't sure what. We rented a cottage in the townland of Annamult, some miles from Bennetsbridge in County Kilkenny. Michael had known Stanley Moss, the miller, when they were both students, and Stanley found us this place.

We bought an ice-cream wagon in Dublin and trundled our belongings on a slow, imperilled journey, in which the car boiled and smoked like a train. The cottage, a three-roomed hovel with no water or electricity, belonged to a Protestant farmer and was up a boreen with foot-deep ruts on either side. Along with the cottage was a barn and a row of outhouses, and in autumn we'd have a drill of potatoes. For this we paid four shillings a week.

Michael was quite happy in this position. His powerful mother disapproved of me and thought me not good enough for her favourite son. My family disapproved of Michael. A perfect beginning!

So he started to write. And me? I bought four bonhams and some pullets, and opened up the field at the back of the haggard for vegetables. I fetched drinking water in a jerry can, established barrels under the gutters for washing, and purchased a Primus stove and a bed, a table and two chairs. The large hearth had a black pot, which hung in the chimney, and I purchased a pot oven in Kilkenny for making bread. My pigs needed skim milk, so I borrowed the neighbour's ass and cart and walked the long miles to and from Bennetsbridge once a week.

The Bardwells came from a long line of shopkeepers – haberdashers all over the English Midlands – and Mick was given an income by his generous mother, in the belief that she was backing a winner in the literary stakes. The pigs were an insurance against future penury when the remittance ran out.

To be a respectable married woman was no easy task for me. I didn't want to be respectable, and I didn't want to be married.

I was bored stupid. I painted the walls of the house and put up posters. I played 'doll's house'. I wanted friends and fun but there were none around. I found that Mick was a recluse, and discouraged visitors. When the Butlers, who lived a few miles away, called, he was downright rude. I was mortified.

I did try. I lied to myself assiduously, broke my back cleaning the sties, digging the garden and milking the goats. Gradually I became spiteful, snappy over the slightest thing. Mick, unaware of my frustrations, worked at his cartoons, wrote a funny account of our disastrous journey in the ice-cream wagon (now sold to some passing innocent) and once in a while sniffed the air at the doorway like a 'real' writer.

In my dilemma, I got pregnant. I thought this was what I should do. But I didn't really think. I wasn't able to think. I was a hopeless case.

Then, God, the discomfort of carrying jerry cans of water, and scouring out the pig sties, weary to death of my condition as my body swelled to outrageous proportions. I could have balanced a tray on the edge of my stomach. And once again the interminable sickness, as was always the case with my pregnancies. On 21 May I gave birth to twins, Billy and Anna.

As I had walked the streets of Birmingham with my load, I had walked the fields of Kilkenny crying out to the birds and animals to save me from this fate I had imposed on myself. I could not develop a motherly persona, make pretty baby clothes, be calm and sedate. I spent many hours sitting on the wall of an old ruined castle nearby, gazing, my eyes turned inwards, looking at nothing.

In this cottage, with no water or electricity, I commenced to breastfeed both the babies. They were good babies, and thrived in this unlikely atmosphere. Mick did his best, changing nappies and holding one while I fed the other. I'd heard of a neighbour who'd had her breast nibbled by a rat while she was asleep, and

I feared I might doze while feeding one of the children. I snapped and roared and wept but continued to feed them for six months. Yes, they were extraordinary. They slept well, like little angels, and I was inordinately proud of them.

There was a feud between the Mosses and the Butlers, Peggy and Hubert. Both families befriended us. The situation called for tact. And when the twins were six months old, the Butlers offered us their house, Maidenhall, as they were going on holiday. Although there was still no electricity in Maidenhall and it was freezing cold, it was a rags-to-riches week. The woman who came in to clean, Mrs Ken, was at our disposal, and she was wonderful with me, and all my strictures about my babies. They must be out in their prams in all weather and have the window open in their room winter and summer. They must not wear rubber knickers in case they got nappy rash. Pissy blankets hung everywhere, and Mrs Ken washed and scrubbed and knelt on the cold stone floors. At night we lit the Aladdin lamp and read more books on rearing babies.

Hubert and Peggy Butler returned unexpectedly a day early. We were in the sitting room. The precious Aladdin had begun to smoke, and just as Hubert entered the mantle flared and burnt. It was my fault: I had turned the mantle up too quickly. I was distraught over this, paralysed with guilt. And afterwards, Hubert got wind that we had entertained Stanley Moss in his house. This was an unforgivable sin. I didn't know where to turn. But the row, which wasn't a row, petered out, and we remained on uneasy terms thereafter.

So, back in our hovel in a long, low winter. Winds howled, rain gushed into the gulleys, and our pullets straggled around the yard, feathers flattened, or perched inside their house, looking out like senior citizens. We cooked on the Primus. We had bacon every day out of the salted barrel. We hoarded our carrots in peat moss; we hung our onions from a string. Our potato harvest had been plentiful. We didn't starve. By seven months, I was exhausted. I put the babies on goats' milk and, as ever, they thrived.

My Aunt Olive had tried to persuade Mick that the babies be baptised. Mick refused. She had sent down christening robes, beautiful old lace garments that had christened many Hones. It was mortifying for me. I had to tell her of Mick's decision. She never forgave me, and she vetoed his ever visiting her house in Malahide. I was too weak to gainsay him. I could have gone along with it. I didn't care one way or the other whether the children were christened, but I didn't want to fall out with my aunt, who had done so much for me. It was the end of my relationship with my beloved aunt.

By now, my father was well settled in his new marriage. As I said, had I stayed with him this might not have happened. He had courted and won a wonderful woman, Valerie Colley, who came from a big family outside Clondalkin. She was the opposite of my mother. She was a real homemaker, a woman who made her own cheese, cooked wonderful meals. My mother had always boasted that she couldn't boil an egg.

So once again my father had fallen on his feet. A lot older than Valerie, he now experienced a comfortable late middle age with very few financial worries, since the house was in effect part of the Colleys' family home. They had owned an enormous mansion called Corkagh, which was subsequently pulled down and the land sold to a speculator. So my father could more or less do what he liked – making bits of furniture, doing house improvements and tending a huge walled garden – with this new woman to cosset him and keep him from harm. They had one son, Christopher.

But back to our situation in Annamult, which was very different from the comfortable home of my father and his new wife. The farmer, our landlord, was the seventh son of a seventh

son. His father had come from the north of Ireland as a jour-
neyman, sleeping in hay barns, scrimping and saving, marrying
and begetting sons. A hard Protestant. A hard man. His eldest
son, our landlord, told me how he had once been making a ken-
nel for a dog and his father had caught him. Such a time-wast-
ing occupation called for extreme punishment. His punishment
was to hang upside-down in the haggard for twenty-four hours.
This tyrant went on to build seven houses for his seven sons –
ugly concrete squares. So our landlord's wife had to produce
seven sons to please her father-in-law. She gave birth to six
daughters in a row, while she milked and churned and slaved
from dawn till dusk. At last she produced a son. I heard after we
left that she went on to produce six more.

It was in Kilkenny that I learnt the saying: 'You never see a
bed-end in a Protestant gap.'

This demonic ethos was disquieting. While I was pregnant, I
had gone to my father's new home for a short break. I had borrowed the family car to go over to Leixlip to see Barney, and
Rosemary. They now had a daughter. My obsession with Barney
had fizzled out, but I got on well with Rosemary, who was a
sophisticate from that other world! She dressed me up and we
went to the Spa Hotel and got drunk. On the Spa hill the car
boiled up, and I was about to go to the hotel for water when a
Guard passed. I vomited on the pavement at his feet. Of course
he smelled the liquor, so he hauled me into the garda station at
Lucan. We were both pulled and dragged along the road and
thrown into a cell. Barney had to come in the middle of the
night to spring us. There was a court case. Our solicitor, Mr
O'Connor, nicknamed 'Mailboat' O'Connor because he had
thrown himself off the mailboat to annoy his mother, was useless. My licence was endorsed for a year. They didn't take your
licence away in those days – unless you killed someone. It was in
all the papers, and the locals read about it. This changed their

attitude towards me. Where was the responsible housewife now? I became a pariah overnight. It was reported in the *Kilkenny People* on the very day I had my first poem published in that paper. It was a terrible poem, and I hope no one ever digs it out of the archives.

My father told me that I was going the way of Nat. Nat was my cousin, the black sheep of the family. My Uncle Joe's son, the very same that had left off the brake of my go-cart in Killiney. He had spent several fortunes on drink and all kinds of badness. He had been sent to Oxford and squandered his father's money, reputedly hiring marquees and holding four-day parties. He had subsequently married a Catholic woman from Cork, had had a rake of kids and had given the eldest to the Butlers to bring up. (They only had one daughter.)

So in a sense I was connected with the Butlers. But where was I in this family circle? I felt that I was a point on the circumference, pinned by circumstance, and might fly off any minute.

In spite of this ostracism, I soldiered on, pretending not to notice the offending stares. Luckily, the Mahers, our immediate neighbours, remained friendly, and we sometimes *ceilidh*ed in their house, dancing to the squeezebox into the small hours.

I had reached a watershed. Nothing seemed to be going right. My interest in the babies simply wasn't enough. Mick and I did not communicate. Life was too fraught. I felt uneducated and damned by it.

I decided to study. I signed on with a correspondence course to do six subjects for the Matric: Latin, French, History, Geography, Maths and English. I needed high marks in five subjects if I was to continue at university. So along with feeding the babies, looking after the pigs and digging the garden, I studied for hours.

We moved house. Another waterless place, although there was a large rainwater tank – which dried up in summer. But compared with Annamult, this was a palace. It had four rooms and a magnificent garden, with apple trees, strawberries and raspberries already growing. My work, mostly at night, progressed. And then it happened. Again.

The week before I was due to go to London to sit the Matric, Christopher arrived to stay with the Butlers. The wheel of coincidence was turning again. As I mentioned before, he and Hubert Butler were old colleagues, and Peggy Butler was one of Christopher's best friends.

My senses could not handle this. I sat on the rainwater tank and wept. Christopher was a drinker. His life filled mine with laughter. We went to the local pub, the three of us. Mick had no notion of my feelings. I sometimes think that Mick lacked a tiny portion of his brain. An enzyme, perhaps, that distorts and orders love. So if he had none, perhaps I had an overdose. In love, I'm a genuinely sick person. Love aborts my intelligence. If I fell in love in a space rocket on the way to the moon, I'd jump out of the capsule.

It was a terrible night. I told Christopher I couldn't live without him. He told me I was married. I had duties: to my children, my husband. I didn't understand what he was talking about. He pushed me away. I wept, as I said, on the rainwater tank, that summer's night, while the birds ruffled their feathers in the fir tree, while stars winked in the cold pewter sky and the planet continued to be.

I passed all the subjects with honours, and when I returned to Kilkenny he was gone.

A couple of months went by, and I planned to run away, or at least have one more try. At what? Being with Christopher for the rest of my life? Poor ingénue that I was, I still hoped for some utopian existence like a lovelorn creature out of a Thomas Hardy novel.

I told Mick I wouldn't be away long, and he decently said he'd mind the babies. How I knew where Christopher lived, I don't know, but I took the boat and went straight to his flat in London. Once again, I spent three nights in his bed but there was no solution. He would never take me on, especially with two children. I returned to Mick, and for a long time afterwards my senses abandoned me.

Then there was more scandal in the local press. Paloma and John came to stay. We were caught drinking after hours in a Bennetsbridge pub. Hubert Butler read me a lecture about drinking in the locality; it was time to go.

Peggy and Hubert drove us to the boat in Waterford, babies, belongings and broken hearts.

PART EIGHT

DIVORCE

190

Five years later, Mick and I got divorced.

Although before this, a lot of grey water would flow under the bridges.

He bought a cottage in a village called Barton outside Cambridge. I began to study Ancient History in correspondence with London University. It was hard going. I did third-level Latin and bored myself stupid reading Cicero and studying Roman law. I had imagined Ancient History would be full of social antiquities. I read Thucydides, which was not on my course. I had to do English and French too that first year. As usual the French was easy, but I had to spend hours writing essays, which I hated.

Another long low winter. Mick was finally running out of money, having breezed through his remittance, so he had to get a job. He went to work at night in a pesticide plant, a shockingly unprotected job. He came home each morning with a yellow face.

We were both tired. I studied half the night, minded the babies, now toddlers, all day. It was a sixteenth-century thatched cottage with wattle walls, very pretty and with a good garden, but a bad experience made me hate the place. One night a prowler came while I was sitting writing an essay. His flat moronic face pressed against the slatted window. I ran to the door with the poker, my heart thumping. He dived away through the bushes and I heard a car starting up on the road.

The next day I spent making curtains and covering all the windows. At night, while Mick was at work, I sat facing the door, ready to jump. I had had a bad shock. I was under strain and my nerves were out of control.

Once again I craved friends, needed companionship badly. I made occasional forays amongst the lecturers at Cambridge, expecting intellectual stimulation, with no success. The last thing they wanted was to talk books with me. I bought a bicycle from a woman, who was bent in half like a paperclip. (The Broads crippled people with rheumatism.) In this anomalous hinge of studying for an extra-mural degree in London while living beside one of the most beautiful universities in the world, I cycled the flat roads of Cambridgeshire.

And poor Mick, returning every night from the chemical factory yellow and bedraggled, had no sweet be-lipsticked wife to greet him with: 'Did you have a terrible day?'

I got as far as Alexander the Great and thought: what the hell? On a crazy impulse, I wrote to John Aitkenhead to ask if I could come back. I knew then that leaving Kilquhanity when we were married had been a mistake. There we had a humorous relationship surrounded as we were with people, but, thrown together on our own, we did not have enough in common to sustain us. The racial difference was more obvious as well. Although one hates to make generalisations, there does seem to be a spontaneousness or volatility in the Celtic temperament which is not necessarily appreciated by the more practical Saxon. Though, indeed, Mick himself was not particularly practical. If anything, I was the more practical of the two, so perhaps 'practical' is not the right word: the more biting epithet, 'cold', might be more appropriate in his case. But whatever it was, after this new move we grew further and further apart.

Meanwhile, I had heard through the grapevine that Christopher was ill. He had contracted TB and was in hospital in London.

I knew I must go to him. I told Mick and once again he kindly agreed to mind the children. I took a train the following day.

It was a mistake. He barely greeted me. Always thin, he was now emaciated. His hollow cheeks, which I had found so attractive, were purple bowls. He looked at me with those great blue eyes.

'Why have you come?' he asked.

'I was worried.'

'No need. They can cure me with streptomycin.'

Treatment was crude. They had deflated one of his lungs and he was clearly in great discomfort.

What was I doing there? Thinking only of myself, I hadn't brought him anything. Not even flowers.

Scalded by the pain of loss, I crept away and, in a worse state than ever, returned to Barton.

John's letter had arrived agreeing to take me and the babies on, so I packed my bags and trundled back to Castle Douglas.

I dropped my studies. They seemed suddenly pointless, too much of an effort. I found the history of wars and politics boring. But now, again, I was taking on an overkill. Working at Kilquhanity, which had never been easy, was now made trebly difficult by having my babies with me.

I became dirty and slovenly, something that always happened when I was unsure of myself. I had been a filthy teenager, with long black nails and straggly hair – which was at one point covered in nits. It was as if I wanted to make myself invisible, or perhaps blend in with the mud that surrounded Leixlip House!

I couldn't cope at all with the group of nursery kids I was asked to take over. And then an escapade with Graham McLachlan. (I had been giving him a Latin grind when I found myself in his bed.) This ended in a miscarriage, which was probably just as well.

I felt myself to be a pariah and I knew that John would have liked to get rid of me. I was more trouble than I was worth. But I obstinately held on.

Eventually Mick came up and, unaware of my one-night – or rather one-day – stand, he made a film of Graham and the children. A sweet film, a record of possible times that never were.

We left Kilquhanity then and went to north Hampstead, where he had bought a house in Weech Road. We both hoped in our different ways that our marriage might mend. He hoped that living in London might prove more to my liking. But once again I was hit by the scourge of boredom and loneliness.

Mick had two brothers: Bill, a composer, and Brian, a journalist. And two sisters: Hillary, who was married to Kingsley Amis, and Margaret, who was married to a nuclear physicist. When the twins were three, Mick suggested that Brian and I should go to Brittany to find a place to stay and that Mick would follow with the twins. Mick had become interested in making 8-millimetre movies, and thought the wild Breton coast might make a good backdrop. Brian was working in UNESCO and living in Paris.

We set off from Victoria Station one sunny morning when the swallows were swooping round the girders. Arriving at St Malo, we hired bicycles and went to look for suitable holiday accommodation for the family. Imagine the freedom as we spun down the roads, sun and shade and fig trees. Speaking French. Eating oysters and drinking cider. What happened was inevitable. We fell into each other's arms, and for a moment the world turned in our favour and Brian, who'd had an unhappy marriage, was equally borne away on wings. We found a friendly *pension* full of working-class Parisians and slept three nights coiled up like puppies.

When Mick and the twins arrived, I had to resume my married status. But with unforgivable cruelty I crept out of his bed, thinking he was asleep, and went down to Brian's room.

It was unforgivable because I was not in love with Brian. It had been a skit, which should have ended there.

All hell broke loose in the Bardwell family.

Thou shalt not take thy brother's wife into thy bed.

Thou shalt not take thy husband's brother into thy bed.

If thou dost this, thou art a thousand times a sinner.

I was now ostracised. A familiar situation. I had done the family, not only Mick, an inestimable wrong.

Cider and oysters in Brittany were no excuse!

PARIS

Paris. All through my childhood and teens, I had wanted to live in Paris. My ultima Thule. So when Brian went back to his job in Paris, I was left stranded in Weech Road, with a furious Mick and the two toddlers, who were now three and a bit. I decided that I could not continue to live with Mick in this situation. He had put up with my obsession with Christopher, which had already splintered our relationship beyond retrieval, and now this. I decided that I would put the children into a nursery and go. I did not allow myself to think of what damage this might do to them. I drove them to the nursery and left them, with the proviso that Mick would visit them once a week.

'Please give me three months,' I begged him.

The reflected sun danced on the hulls of the boats in Calais harbour. Dock workers in their denim overalls pulled at the hawsers, hurled barrels, trundled trolleys with cardboard packages containing hardware.

The air was sleepy and forgiving.

Autumn came greyly to the Paris streets. We lived in one room, sharing a kitchen with a journalist next door. Post-war France was in turmoil. Poverty was rife. The clochards slept on the open grids above the Metro lines for a little warmth. They slept all day and wandered the streets at night. There was no work for me. I queued every morning for translation work, to no avail. I sold a student rag, walking the streets, the gendarmes telling me to 'Move on! Move on!' I was told to cry: '*C'est ni communiste ni catholique!*' GIs lounged about and sometimes bought a copy of the paper or would take me to a café, hoping to 'make it' with me. I drank the coffee greedily but ran away afterwards. Graffiti on the walls and bridges: 'Americans go HOME'.

Food was dear. If I made a pound a day, I fed myself; if I didn't, I went hungry. The journalist had lost his job freelancing for two papers that were politically poles apart, so he spent his days in the flat, filling up forms and getting nowhere. He taught me to eat raw donkey mince with garlic and potatoes and to drink the potato water, for the vitamins. That was how he kept himself alive. I went round with a consumptive Marseillais who took me to his friends the rag dealers. He was fascinated by my use of the subjunctive. He used to tell them I was in Paris '*pour perfectioner la langue française*'. The ordinary paper sellers had stands. I envied them not having to walk about. They were good to me, however, and when it rained they gave me cover for my journal. And the chestnut sellers gave me chestnuts for free. I can still taste them and feel their gorgeous texture.

Brian did not earn enough money to support two people. November came in very cold, and there was no heating in the flat. We huddled under blankets at night, and I walked the streets all day. The paper, which consisted of ridiculous articles and poems in the style of Jaques Prevert, came out once a month, and it was almost impossible to sell after the first week. And anyway, the Parisians were poor and had no money to waste on such a rag. (Eventually we sellers used to shout: '*C'est ni communiste, ni catholique, ni Prevert!*')

I was anaemic, having lost two stone, but I would not give up on Paris. I was in the city of my dreams, even though they now had a nightmarish quality. I read Beckett in French and discovered his Hiberno-French. Strange reading about Dublin's Grand Canal in the middle of Paris!

Mick sent me photos of the twins, increasing my guilt. The journalist asked me who they were, and I answered: 'Oh, just some kids of a friend of mine.'

Naturally, then I got pregnant. I could not continue in this starving state. At least, it was not far off starving. I tried stealing food but was nearly caught. I lived on a doughy cake, the cheapest thing you could buy. It stuck to the roof of your mouth but it was food.

I had done my three months in Paris. I had walked the length and breadth of it. I knew it. I still loved it. But now I had to go home. Go home to my twins, to my uneasy life with Mick – and bring my load with me.

I think Mick was more upset that I was pregnant than that our relationship was out the window. He said he would have liked us to have another child.

'You never told me that,' I said.

'You never asked.'

I craved affection as though it were an item to be found on a market stall. I made a bid for it then. I asked him to take me back. I laid my head on his chest, my arms round his neck. 'No,' he said. He was happy with his relationship with his new friend. She was his cousin. (Mick's parents had been first cousins. The Bardwells kept within their clan! Yet who was I to talk, having been down that same road.)

The twins were traumatised from their stay away, especially Billy. And all that winter I sat with them in a bedroom while they fought and pulled each other's hair. As usual I was sick and dreadfully tired. The doctor put me on iron injections and vitamin B. He said my blood count was dangerously low.

In January 1952, Brian gave up his job and came to London. So Brian and I and the twins moved out of Weech Road and found a flat in Carleton Road, near Holloway. A cold, inhospitable flat, but it was cheap. It was actually a maisonette, and shortly we sublet to a Dutch family called Wibaut. They had children – two the same age as Anna and Billy – and Mr Wibaut had two wives, one in the country and one there. The country one knew nothing of the town one, but since he 'travelled in' gherkins and pickled eggs, this arrangement was perfect for him!

Having another family upstairs suited us well. Inveigling the Wibauts into summer excursions out of London, we searched the coast for camping places. I often set out alone with the children on spec, arriving late at some seaside resort. On one occasion I woke up in a car park with an Alsation in the tent and a furious policeman saying 'You can't camp 'ere.' We toured the south coast or sometimes went further afield, to Cornwall. My daughters were real water babies, and Anna used to spend hours collecting what she called 'Precious stones' – the smoothed-over bits of coloured glass that littered the stony beaches.

At the back of the so-called garden, a wasteland of rubbish, stood the gaunt edifice of Holloway Jail. At night one could hear the women screaming. Blood-curdling wails into the small hours. Later I learnt that the screams were prearranged by a rota to discomfort the screws. The warders were enormous women, with turf-like shoulders, who could be seen parading in the street in front of the crenellated portals (which were designed, I believe, to look like Warwick Castle).

William Bardwell, the composer and self-styled dilettante, who looked on me as a waste of time, had composed tiny jumpy pieces called 'Oscarias' for a man who could whistle in thirds. This person was called Oscar Gates.

He lived with his new woman, Maggie, and their daughter Liza in a house in Hargrave Park, a street off Holloway Road. They had a tiny flat at the top of the house with no electricity, only gas lighting. And at one stage, bed bugs tormented them, and they had to get the de-infestation squad round to delouse them. In fact, they had to delouse the whole street. Bugs would live behind the wallpaper and come out at night. He described them dropping off the wall on to the bed with a thump.

Oscar worked for British Rail in Euston Station in an office called 'Inward Fish'. He had worked in the Foreign Office after leaving college but, being a communist, couldn't stand his colleagues and decided to join the working classes. We were all communists in those days, or at least fellow travellers. (He is 'Maximillian' in my novel *That London Winter.*)

The Bardwells were a musical family: Mick was a fine pianist, and Brian played the flute. So it was through Bill that we met this strange man, and his partner.

The divorce between me and Mick went through smoothly. He was now shacked up with his cousin Mary, whom he intended to marry. I often wondered whether Mick thought he was well shut of me. His mother was probably the only person whom he really loved, and since Mavy Bardwell disliked me, it left the way open for her to take him back into the emotional nest.

Paloma Says Goodbye

After a while, it seemed like a good idea for us all to go to Ireland. My father had sold the house in Leixlip and, as I said, married Valerie and moved into their beautiful home off the Naas Road. So I brought Billy and Anna and Jacky there for a visit. My daughter, Jacky, had been born the previous August and was a tiny tot.

Paloma had now divorced John Price and had left her youngest child, Deirdre, in Westmeath. Gail was with her. She had plans. One was to leave Gail with our Aunt Olive, and Deirdre with her paternal grandmother, and set sail for a new life.

She had met a man who knew how to cadge a lift on a trading vessel which would take them to South Africa. They duly boarded the boat in Hull. And a hazardous journey it was. They spent weeks on treacherous seas, nearly capsized in the Bay of Biscay, and finally arrived at their destination emaciated but lucky to have survived. Thence she went to Zimbabwe (then Southern Rhodesia), with the idea of milking the last of the British Empire – when there were still jobs reserved for the whites. She soon found a new man, married him and settled down to join the racing establishment, subsequently riding on the flat herself.

But nothing ever lasted with Paloma. In spite of her brilliant horsemanship, her beauty and her egotism – which amounted to total self-belief – all her jobs and relationships seemed to run into cul-de-sacs. (Before she died, she had ploughed through three more husbands.)

It was not until the sixties that she paid a last visit to Ireland. By that stage she had become unpleasantly racist and embarrassing to be with. But she never lost her charisma.

So there, on the lawn of my father's house, I bid my sister farewell. She hugged my father – how they still loved each other – but the parting wasn't tragic for him, because he was so content with his new life. As for the two of us, we had parted ways a long time ago. We seemed to have nothing in common any more.

As a child, I had adored her; as a teenager, I had envied her; and as an adult, I'd become a smart-arsed intellectual and imagined that I was well beyond her in the fields of culture. Although it has to be admitted that she still held a certain amount of emotional authority over me. For myself, embarked as I was on a complex life of uncontrolled chaos, I seemed to have lost the capacity for unselfish love. And I had not grown up: I still lived in the emotional midden of early childhood. So it was with the meanest feeling of impatience that I waited for her to go.

Thus, in this way, her two daughters, Gail and Deirdre (my Aunt Olive wouldn't hear of her being left in Westmeath, and changed her name to Anne, because of the tragic connotations of the name Deirdre), grew up in comparative luxury but without either of their parents.

Having seen my sister away and, for all these ambiguities, wishing her well, I hung around for a week or so, incognito, as it were – not being able to admit that my divorce was pending and that Jacky wasn't Mick's child – and enjoying the clean air and comfort, before returning to London, Brian, and the precarious future that was looming.

202

PART NINE
CARLETON ROAD

But to go back to the beginnings of our stay in Carleton Road with Brian and the twins, our friendship with Oscar and Maggie was already cemented. And the way these things happen, Brian and I and Maggie and Oscar became a foursome. Every other night, one of the couples cooked the meal. Oscar and I talked and laughed, and Maggie and Brian played a supporting role. In a short time, it was clear the way things were going.

Nothing worked in our flat. The cistern wheezed, the bath geyser was dangerously old, the gas cooker had just one working flame and was encrusted with grease. In my usual way, I set about painting walls and putting up shelves. So to this inhospitable place, Oscar and Maggie came every other night.

I had met Brian in Waterloo Station and somehow realised that once more I had made a mistake. The glistening aura of Paris had left him – the Boul' Mich and Odéon, Montmartre and Montparnasse – places where I'd hung around hoping for a glimpse of Jean-Paul Sartre or Camus. In dark, polluted London in midwinter, there was nothing to make the adrenalin leap. So Oscar and Maggie were to become the catalyst.

The twins, traumatised as they were (especially Billy) by their stay in the nursery, were disorientated further by the move to Carleton Road. Once again, my pregnancy took its toll. As often happens to babies in this situation, they refused to eat. I'd get worked up about this, and my neurotic anxiety did more harm than good.

Maggie had one of those high-cheek-boned handsome English faces, and I admired her greatly. She was a good draughtsperson, had studied at Norwich, where she'd met and married her husband. She had two other children, who only came part-time from their father. Oscar was around six foot tall, with almost rabbinical features and a nest of thick brown hair, which he brushed to one side of his head. He walked proudly with a slight backwards tilt. I was fascinated by both of them.

But what I was about to do was to betray a fine woman and a decent man. During my pregnancy, which continued into a warm summer, Oscar and I saw much of each other. I trailed around to museums and longed again for the freedom of my body. But it was not until after Jacky was born, on 3 August 1952, that we got to know each other in the Biblical sense.

Oscar was obsessed with sex, music and politics – in that order. Every afternoon, with Jacky in the carrycot in the back of an old car, and with the twins now at school up the road, we'd circle outlying spots of Hampstead for bombed-out houses. Climbing up rickety staircases, we'd lie on the bare boards making love till it was time for me to fetch the twins, and for Oscar to go home to Maggie. His working hours – from six till two every day – fitted into the jigsaw of betrayal perfectly. Brian worked on the *Daily Express*, where he'd got a job on the foreign desk.

Every month, Oscar worked a week of night duty. I'd fly down to Euston on my bike and we'd climb up in among machinery and packages to make ourselves a bed of coats and blankets.

In the afternoons, when I went to fetch him in my ancient car (I always seemed to manage to acquire a wheezing machine),

I'd park in Eversholt Street and he'd be on the roof of the station whistling a Bach prelude or fugue with his perfect pitch. We did other things as well as making love, though. We used to go to the gramophone exchange in Wardour Street and sit in the booth listening to all kinds of music, from Mahler to Couperin, from modern pop to New Orleans jazz. We hardly ever bought a record, but to excuse ourselves we'd buy a packet of needles for our wind-up gramophones. Neither of us could afford to buy what was then called a 'pick-up'. I was the first of the two of us to get one: a black box which played LPs and forty-fives. I bought Buddy Holly and the Platters. We joined the Cine Club under Waterloo Bridge and saw all the modern French films, especially the Cocteaus, one after the other as they were released. We watched Carmen Jones and old classics like *The Wages of Fear*, with Yves Montand. We'd spend hours in Foyle's second-hand book department making up ditties and giggling over potential thefts.

He spoke elegant French, as I did, and we'd put the language on and off like a worn coat. We thought highly of ourselves, the new moderns, the new sophisticates, the new intellectuals. I depended on him both sexually and mentally. As far as my emotions were concerned, they remained untapped. My experience with Christopher had been one of extreme pain. Oscar minded me. He had dragged me out of a morass, and although what we were doing was hurting two decent people, we selfishly insulated ourselves from guilt.

He cultivated the new wave of West Indians, who had arrived in England after the war. Many of his co-workers were black, and he'd invite them to Hargravia, as we called it – the slum in north London – maintaining in this way a semblance of family life with Maggie and Liza. He believed that black people knew how to use their bodies, unlike the inhibited English, whom he despised.

There was a lightness in me once again. My skin shone. I dressed extravagantly, making my own and my children's clothes. I made the little girls lovely frocks from ends of material, and Jacky and his Liza, who was just a year older, became inseparable and remained so for many years.

In the harsh London winters, of fog and frost, it was more difficult to find bombed-out buildings to break into, so instead we hired a small room near Euston Station. A young man who had become interested in Maggie became obsessed with the notion of having me as well. He found our hideout and followed me there one day when Oscar was at work. It was a terrible betrayal to Oscar. But I, always expecting to be the one to be hurt, never believed that I could hurt others.

SOHO

This young man had trawled Soho and began to tell me about various people he had met there. Artists and writers, all famous, all illustrious – all, one way or another, drinking themselves to death.

Soho wasn't entirely new to me. Oscar and I frequently went to cafés to drink the new espresso coffee or have tea in the French café at the corner of Frith Street. But Oscar didn't drink. In fact, he abhorred drunkenness, so we never ran into these people on our excursions.

This young man brought me to the French pub in Dean Street. There was a buzz in the place. I imagined that this was where I'd meet the 'real' people – the artists and writers with whom I instinctively knew I belonged.

The first people I talked to were the two Roberts, Robert McBryde and Robert Colquhoun. McBryde, tidy and dark, with eyes as inquisitive as a feral cat's, could charm the most sullen with his songs and laughter. He knew a rake of Scottish airs, 'The Three Marys' being his favourite. Colquhoun, on the other hand, tall and conventionally handsome, and troubled of feature, was wary of McBryde's easy popularity. Of the two, he was considered the more important artist, although McBryde was no mean painter, and a few of his still lifes which hang in Glasgow have stood the test of time.

They seduced me with their wit and charm. Others followed. We roamed up Dean Street and entered the Club de Caves de France. The barman, Secundo, brother of the boxer Primo Carnera, was the master of this domain. The owner, a sharp-eyed French woman, was nursemaid and general keeper-in-check to all her customers, whom she knew by their Christian names. That same day, I met Anthony Cronin and his wife Therese.

One thing I hadn't realised that I'd missed all these years was the Celtic temperament. With the Roberts – Scottish – and the Cronins – Irish – something inside me was released. I found the Cronins, with their great wit and energy, enormously exciting, and I felt that I wanted to spend time with them night and day. And they knew *everybody*. Francis Bacon. George Barker, like a sexy tortoise, nicknamed 'the Master'. His wife Elizabeth, the writer of *By Grand Central Station I Sat Down and Wept*. Peter Brooke, alias Anthony Carson, who wrote a witty column for the *New Statesman and Nation*. Paul Potts. And Anthony Burgess. And I was a nobody. A *Protestant* nobody at that!

I still went out with Oscar in between these now-almost-nightly forays into Soho. I wanted to present myself with this intelligent, handsome escort, but this didn't suit him at all. He hated what he considered messing, and I had dived into the mess like a porpoise after salmon.

I was smitten by the Roberts and the Cronins, how they lived every tick of the clock, how Tony managed to write poems and reviews for the *Times*, and still seemed to play twenty-four hours a day. And most of all I was smitten with this whirlwind life. It was like taking part in a circus, walking the high wire without a safety net, taming wild animals, and being part of a team. With the Wibauts upstairs as resident babysitters, I was free to roam once the children were in bed. Dressed up in my swanky clothes and my cheap jewellery, I'd go to the French Pub, on Dean Street, or 'the Caves'.

Oscar and I began to fight. Sometimes he'd cycle away from me. I'd follow him, shouting, and he'd laugh, saying it was like 'The Ride of the Valkyrie'. He started standing me up. One sordid February day, on my birthday, we had arranged to meet at the Odeon at Camden Town and he didn't show. I was devastated. This man with whom I'd been so secure for nearly seven years, who had reinstated me as a member of the human race, had ceased to need me.

Hampstead proliferated with sturdy intellectuals, and he joined a musical society on his own. Before, we would have done this together. I knew there were hundreds of frustrated women in these societies, women who masturbated away their lost souls, who'd need an Oscar for their bodies and their minds. And I knew *he* knew that too.

So I courted the Cronins assiduously for their wild, extravagant ways. I wanted a troupe of my own.

While I was with Oscar, I had hardly written a word. But now, the writing began to flow again. Poems and short stories. Yet I dared not show them to anyone.

Anthony Cronin, with his easy laugh, impressed me most, especially his scholarship and literary knowledge. I was pleased when I could pick up on his references from Beckett or Joyce, for example. I had loved his book *The Life of Riley*, finding it an intriguing portrait of Dublin bohemian life. He had been editor of *The Bell* then, and I had sent him a story just as the magazine folded. I knew nothing of Dublin adult life, having grown up in my solitary way, and, with my young life having been 'knifed' by my pregnancy and enforced exile, I had lost an important year.

So here was a man who filled in those Irish years as the centre of a coterie of literati in the Dublin of the forties and early fifties. His endearing personality, made manifest by his sense of humour, made him an exceptional companion. He had a difficult time, however: he was always broke, and was always just managing to keep his wife and child fed and the rent paid. The fact that he managed to write anything in that chaotic atmosphere is nothing short of miraculous.

I had not known the Roberts in their heyday, but when I met them they were living off Colquhoun's early reputation (and McBryde's ability to entertain). And they, too, were always broke. Yet without the Roberts, that era in Soho would never have been the same.

There was the Colony Rooms, where Bacon and various poets went. This was more exclusive than the Caves. I couldn't believe how old Bacon was – well over fifty – since he looked barely twenty-five. I didn't go there much, but I remember the canary, which was the centre of attention. The Roberts were not allowed in, not even when Colquhoun had a large retrospective exhibition at the Whitechapel Gallery in the late fifties.

This exhibition, which featured many large canvasses, had a mixed reception, with the inevitable comparison with Picasso. Naturally anyone who was at art college in the thirties must have been influenced by Picasso, yet there was a poetic quality about his drawings, especially, that was entirely his own. It was a hard time for him, though, as he had once been the talk of the town, along with John Minton and others.

I remember that when we got back from the exhibition, the proprietress of the Caves asked: 'Has Colquhoun got to the "Give me a whisky" stage?'

We had travelled back by bus, myself and McBryde, both the Roberts penniless. Colquhoun told me that when he woke up the following day he didn't even have a shilling for the gas. So he couldn't get a glass of hot water, never mind a cup of tea. McBryde, jealous of Colquhoun's brief lionisation, had disappeared in a huff.

You couldn't but love them both. There was a great kindness in them, and I was personally grateful for this, especially as I was someone with no credentials, either literary or artistic. If you were married into the milieu, you were safe. In fact, in that predominantly male society, it was almost better this way. But a single woman on her own, relying solely on her looks and personality, could easily become a target. Being Irish was a help, but being from a Protestant background was a disadvantage. If I could have acted the grande dame, it might have helped, but that sort of thing was anathema to me. So I was easily teased and taunted when a target was needed. But like a child who says 'Please play with me', I always bounced back, to listen and learn, hiding my hurt or lack of confidence.

Yes indeed, it was an all-male society. As an unpublished writer, you were ruled, bedevilled, damned – especially if you were a woman. In all those years, I never got to know either a woman writer or a woman artist. I once met Edith Sitwell, an extraordinary-looking woman, with a head like an eagle, long and lanky, dressed from top to toe in black lace and jewellery. She was holding court on a throne at a party given by the Guinnesses, to which I somehow got invited. But then the Sitwells didn't drink around Soho. They were far too rich and snobbish for that. So in order to keep one's head high, one had to have the strength of a lion and the determination of a fool.

It is possible also that the men who were only holding on by the skin of their teeth were the cleverest at throwing out barbs – or, to use the current jargon, knew exactly which buttons to press. A remark like 'You're only a Protestant, how could you know', said with cruel innuendo, could nearly crucify you. Many's the flood of tears that followed such a comment.

But there were some who never indulged themselves in such petty contempt, who enjoyed your intelligence, your gaiety, your energy. Such a one was Anthony Carson, alias Peter Brooke – or perhaps it was the other way round – a giant of humour and perspicacity. A big bear of a man who laughed constantly, and when he laughed his shoulders bucked with a *hmph-hmph-hmph*. His regular column in the *Statesman* barely kept him alive. He was a very comic writer, very popular, and somehow or other he managed to churn it out longhand, week after week.

These were the people whom I got to know best in this seemingly star-spangled coterie of artists and writers. Alcohol, with which I had been abstemious for so long, became a let-out, or a let-off. It induced a surge of adrenalin which made me, I thought, a witty and imaginative companion. Yet, as I have said, I was never sure of myself.

Then there were others, part-time boozers. Harry Diamond, a young Jew whose only claim to fame was that a portrait of him painted by Lucien Freud hung in Liverpool Art Gallery. And of course Paul Potts. (Although he was a full-time boozer.) Paul was a strange man, very severe, very pure. His book *Dante Called Her Beatrice* had once reached cult proportions but was then almost forgotten. He always sat in the back of the French pub like a Buddha, making the odd cynical remark, and was not without humour. The blind poet John Heath-Stubbs and the deaf poet David Wright, the former crashing into lampposts, the latter waving his hands and laughing soundlessly. John had once mistaken my skirt for a towel when we were standing beside a washbasin!

Long before I was seduced by the Soho milieu, Brian and I had been walking down Shaftsbury Avenue when we were importuned by a well-dressed tramp. He wanted half a crown. He had an upper-class accent, a bent walk, and one shoulder higher than the other. A good-looking man in his fifties. He had nowhere to live. He often slept in the Soho graveyard, a popular place amongst the homeless. We brought him home that night.

This was Napper. Sir Napper Dean Paul, a morphine addict. In those days, we were not used to hard drugs, having barely experimented with marijuana or purple hearts – uppers and downers all in one. When I tried them, they induced in me uncontrolled shaking, so one day, walking down the street, I threw them into the traffic.

Oscar, also, inclined to befriend derelicts, had his own hanger-on. The Countess Eileen, who combed the dustbins outside the Savoy for dancing shoes and the like. You could order garments from her, and she always came up with the goods. Then there was Sylvia, thin as fuse wire, who reclined on the sofa like Madame Récamier, smoking cheroots and telling of her various famous lovers in the past, one of whom had been Augustus John. All these post-aristocratic derelicts took up a lot of time, and needed much personal attention. (These people are to be found, in fictionalised form, in my novel *That London Winter*.)

Once in, Napper had no intention of moving out. He had a long history of morphine addiction, as had his sister Brenda. In the late twenties and thirties, they considered themselves '*les enfants dorés*'. According to Napper, their mother, a beautiful Russian lady, had married a concrete baron. And they had lived amongst the rich and reckless, sliding down the bannisters of their big house in Mayfair, in a Proustian atmosphere. Napper, again according to his story, had had a bad motor accident in his youth, fracturing his skull, and had started taking morphine for the pain. He soon became addicted to it. His sister Brenda, like Elizabeth in Cocteau's *Les Enfants Terribles*, soon followed suit and started injecting herself as well. He described how much they loved each other and how they would 'zip themselves up' with the drug. Gradually they spent their inheritance, clinging to their dependence on each other. Although Napper had married and had a crazy wife somewhere – with a live-in lover half her age. So by the time we met him, he was full of resentment towards both sister and wife, claiming that they both had money stashed away but wouldn't give him a penny.

One didn't know whether to believe his stories or not, although they turned out to be largely true. He had been in and out of jail for possession and had undergone a number of 'cures'. He described vividly the horrors of going cold turkey: the excruciating stomach cramps and the rat-like visions. By now, he had a prescription on the National Health – which was not nearly enough. Hence his getting into trouble with the law. He also occasionally worked for a prostitute in London, beating up colonels and suchlike when she went to Lyon's Corner House for a cup of tea.

He was a nuisance, with his constant whining, his dirt and his needles. Furthermore, he developed a sort of passion for me. He didn't approve of alcohol and was profoundly jealous when I started palling up with new Soho friends. One day he took an overdose, timing it to when he knew I'd be returning, so that I'd save him. He was on the point of collapse but not yet in a coma. I had to haul him into a taxi and deliver him to the hospital to have his stomach pumped. It had been an overdose of Nembutal (not morphine), which he took to make him sleep. They fixed him up all right, but then he began to blame me – as though I'd promised to marry him and had let him down – and declared his undying love. This was a complication I did not need. When he came back, it was an uneasy time. Eventually he found somewhere else, after a short sojourn with Oscar and Maggie.

My rows with Oscar were becoming more and more vicious. I didn't realise at the time that he, like Napper, was jealous of my newfound friends. The Cronins had a flat near Camden Town, and one night when I was going round there, Oscar accompanied me to the door, saying: 'I'm delivering you to the enemy.' It was the first time it had occurred to me that I might be hurting his feelings: since there was no sexual relationship with any of these people, I couldn't understand why he'd mind. But of course, as usual, I let things run on the rails of stupidity.

I was very upset about the turn our relationship was taking. But, as is often the way with fate, I think I just then really fell in love with him, while still not being able to abjure the Soho scene.

Perhaps it was then, and only then, that my tormenting obsession with Christopher ended. He only had to appear out of the blue – a habit he had – to pull at the rags of my heart again. But with all this chaos of Soho, and Oscar's uncertainty towards our relationship, he became desperately important to me, while I became less important to him. He'd had enough. He was prepared to look elsewhere. Now it was my turn to be suspicious. I became obsessed with the suspicion that he might be going out with someone else. He assured me that this was not so, and that he was trying to patch up his relationship with Maggie.

One night, determined to find out the truth, I went to Hargrave Park to see if his scooter was there. (He had a Lambretta.) There was no sign of the bike. Drunk and prostrated with grief, I went up on to the railway line at Tufnell Park and walked along the sleepers, hoping that a goods train might run me over. I muttered under my breath lines by John Betjeman: 'Rumble under, thunder over, midnight bound for Cricklewood.' At that time, there didn't seem to be any point to my life. I felt that I had made a complete mess of everything and that everyone would be better off without me. My children, even, were being neglected by my continuous search for God-knows-what.

But no train came. I was arrested and sent to Marylebone Police Station, from which Brian had to spring me. I was given a mug of tea with 'EIIR' on it, fined five pounds, along with the other drunks and prostitutes, and brought home like a delinquent teenager. *Was I not a mother? Did I not have any responsibility towards my family? What did I think I was doing?* But like a hound unable to resist a flock of sheep, I was back in Soho a few nights later.

I first met Patrick Kavanagh in the Caves. It was Tony who introduced us. He seemed extraordinary to me. I quoted a line of his poetry to him, and he was gleeful. He had the effect of making you think that you were on the verge of some great discovery. He was charming, and delighted to be in London with his peers. He always felt that he was better treated in London than in Dublin. Ill health and poverty had taken its toll, though. He had suffered greatly from the sneers and slights of the Irish Establishment, and consequently had a name for being unmanageable and garrulous. He was comical, but also a little frightening. Having read and admired his poetry, I was in awe of him.

Until now, George Barker had held the poetry throne in Soho, with his large output, his many wives and his sex appeal, but with the arrival of Kavanagh there was a subtle change in the air. Unlike Barker, Kavanagh inspired a reverential attitude from his admirers, and was regarded as a man not to be tampered with. As much as he hated the way he was treated at home, he hated more any suspicion of sycophancy. Whereas the more flattery Barker got, the better he thrived.

Underneath, Kavanagh was in fact a very humble person. He never boasted about his poetry, saying that there had been no one on Parnassus since Homer. He claimed that he had never said 'I am a poet' – which many a lesser poet would assert. Strangely, the only thing I ever heard him boast about was *Tarry Flynn*: he claimed that it was the only real Irish novel that had ever been written. Certainly his comicality and his sadness are equally balanced in that book. And it is now, rightly, considered a classic.

A few nights after our paths had first crossed, we met outside the Cronins' door after ferreting our various ways home, and he began to kiss me like any lover. What Kavanagh presented as his public persona was the opposite of what he was in reality. How else could he have been such a fine poet? In public, also, he presented a virginal, don't-touch-me aura, but in person he was cosy and loving. He loved all women and believed that God must be a woman.

Eventually, Carleton Road became the centre of hospitality: 'The last outpost of civilisation', as Kavanagh described it. The Cronins moved in upstairs – the Wibauts, unable to stand the racket and parties, having moved out. Odds and ends arrived from Dublin. Paddy Ryan, brother of John Ryan, who edited the *Dublin Magazine*. Connor O'Millain, an alcoholic former bank manager. Ray Cortez, a junkie; and a man who called himself a World Citizen and who had played the boats with various gambling games. (Later, they both committed suicide.) Perhaps one of the strangest guests of all was a young Greek boy called Peter Panay – about twelve or thirteen years old – who appeared, seemingly out of nowhere, and before long became part of the 'family'. He used to come in every morning and immediately set to clearing up the previous night's debris, making tea and with great courtesy helping anyone who needed sustenance, physical or mental. He said to me one day: 'When I grow up, I will buy a castle in the country where you will all be able to live, and I will look after you.' So enamoured was he of our so-called bohemian existence.

This was all hard for the children, and terrible for Brian. Coming home late at night from his evening on the foreign desk at the *Express*, he'd find bottles and bodies strewn around the flat. I am not proud of this, I simply record it: it happened. Often, I'd have climbed in with one of the bodies, on a mattress or on the bare boards themselves.

It was a crescendo of madness. It was 1959. This particular era was coming to an end.

But what of Christopher? He had qualified as a psychiatrist, but didn't practise. He had inherited money from his mother and had bought two houses in Spain, which he was renting out. I suppose that, as I have hinted, because of my relationship with Oscar, my crazy seduction by Soho, I had become immunised from my distressful passion for this man, which at any moment might have flared up again. Probably aware of this, he sought me out from time to time. He'd take me to the local pub and we'd drink and laugh the night away. He suffered terribly from arthritis and was partly crippled by it. In a way, I flaunted these relationships with this motley crew of artists and writers at him. Childish, it was, to say the least, because deep down the scar of loss would never heal. So he came and he went. I don't know how he found out where I was living. There must have been a deep bond between us that all the circumstances of our lives could never quite sever. Yet in spite of, or because of, all this, it was Oscar I needed now – and Oscar I was losing.

One afternoon, while we were both cycling down Holloway Road, we stopped at a corner. We started shouting at each other. I screamed and screamed accusations of infidelity, till he told me to fuck off. This is exactly what I did. I got on my bike and cycled away, intending never to see him again.

That same night, dressed in my regalia, I went down to the French pub and met Finton McLachlan.

PART TEN

SOMETHING TO DO WITH SKIN

During the fifties, my grandfather Willie Collis had died and left me some money. A solicitor, he had accumulated a fair bit of property. Like all solicitors, he knew when and where to buy. He was a fair man and divided up his fortune equally between his three sons and his remaining daughter, my Aunt Joyce. My mother's lot was divided equally between myself, Noll and Paloma.

With this considerable wealth – actually about £5,000 in bits and pieces (a fortune – a year's money for a top salaried worker in those days) – I'd draw money from the bank and water anyone who happened to be passing. It was enjoyable, and we seemed to laugh all day at some unaccountable joke.

We continued to use everything that London, especially Soho, offered in those heady post-war years. If the twenties, in theory, were dominated by the Charleston and champagne, the fifties seemed inextricably linked with hard liquor and cerebral gymnastics. Who was the cleverest, who the funniest?

My landlady, Mrs Citovitch, a half-crazy aristocrat who dressed in rags (and who had an even more ragged sister whose husband was certified), lived with a shuffling White Russian who hardly ever got out of his pyjamas. She and her sister had a daughter apiece, Rose and Mitzi. Rose was an ebullient extrovert, Mitzi sour and shy. Mrs Citovitch, who lived beneath us, began to complain about the noise from our flat, saying that she feared that the ceiling would fall on her head. We laughed at her and offered her a drink. In fact, we paid no heed to her. The house might fall any day: what did we care? In any case, they lived in squalor themselves. They are all in my play *Thursday*.

Patrick Kavanagh, now installed in Carleton Road, slept on an ex-army bed in the sitting room. This is where he first met Katherine Moloney.

Katherine Moloney was an Irishwoman who had known the Cronins for years. She was a worker: she had a nine-to-five job in an accountancy firm. She had a certain steadiness of mind and discipline that was lacking in the rest of us at the time. She came from a strong nationalist family. I introduced her to Kavanagh.

Although Kavanagh gleefully accepted the craziness and adulation he encountered in London, as I've said, he really didn't like the bohemian way of life. Yet one night at a party, he asked Katherine into his bed. I persuaded her to join him. 'Go on,' I said. 'He's very nice.' Like me, she was in awe of Kavanagh, but I had experienced his gentleness. 'Come on,' he said to her, 'I won't ate you.'

The result was astonishing. Nobody had paid much heed to Kavanagh's invitation. And when Katherine squeezed herself on to Kavanagh's narrow couch, there seemed to be a kind of hiatus in the all-round hilarity. In fact, the party, probably sensing that they should be left in peace, quietly disbanded.

This was the beginning of a long love affair, which ended in their marriage. (Later, I became very proud of my matchmaking abilities!) The couple were inseparable over the next few weeks, holding hands like teenagers.

Katherine was a good anchor for him. She was generous, good fun, reliable and solid, with lots of energy to spare. And for the next five years, whenever he was in London, he lived with her as man and wife. I can say, quite truly, that he loved her.

She managed him like a child, and kept him well dressed. At home in Ireland, he had neglected himself, but he loved his new sartorial persona. When he was back in Ireland, they'd correspond, and he'd read out her letters. 'Katherine writes a great letter,' he'd say, turning back over the pages. Once, when he was in her London flat, Katherine told him that if the landlord phoned, he must say he was Mister Moloney. He was delighted, recounting this story to all and sundry.

From this period in London, I peopled my novel *That London Winter*. It was a hectic, funny, wonderful and painful period – all these emotions stretched to their limits.

Before my final row with Oscar, there had been a minor episode which upset me dreadfully. There was a beautiful woman called Lilly Heidsieck. She had married into the champagne family but lived with a sculptor, a gentle giant who made tiny figurines. She was half-Greek and had a romantic history, having been part of the Yugoslav resistance during the war: she was one of the 'fighting sixty-nine'.

She seemed like someone you'd meet in a back bar in the Berlin of the twenties. On one of the rare occasions when Oscar agreed to accompany me to Soho, he met and fell for Lily. She was older than me, and much more experienced in the field of international seduction. One night I came to our hideaway and found the two of them in bed. I ranted and threw things and left them to it. I went through the next few weeks in a daze of bewilderment. How had I let this happen? I couldn't pick myself out of my frozen state. He hung around with Lily and the sculptor, setting up exhibitions and running errands for them on his scooter. The affair fizzled out, of course. She was not an easy woman, and I gather that she refused him sexually. But for me, my senses couldn't cope. This was before my abortive suicide attempt, before I realised that I was heading down the corridor of self-destruction.

Oscar never stayed with his women long. In fact, I may have been one of the longest-lasting girlfriends. He often told people afterwards that I was the only one who understood his music. We'd had an ongoing conversation for nearly seven years, and he was probably the only fixed point in my life – perhaps the only person I really cared for in an adult way. But my Lolita-like passion for Christopher – not to mention my non-relationship with my mother – had been far more damaging to my self-esteem.

How can I explain my constant running, my constant searching? Revenge on my mother, who had reneged on me? My superfluity of energy? My desperate need for affection? All puny reasons. To prove that I could 'pull' the men in this senseless odyssey, until I must finally reach the watershed of masochism – out of which I would at last be able to reincarnate myself as a woman of substance. Did I have to find the ultimate sadist, then, until the balance was met?

The night after that fatal row, as I said, I met Finton McLachlan. Finton was something else. He was possibly the most beautiful young man I'd ever seen. With reddish hair, green eyes and golden skin, he was the farthest thing from a 'Paddy' you'd ever meet.

I scooped him up and brought him home. The following day I decided, on the spur of the moment, to go to Dublin. I farmed out my children and we took the Tube to the edge of London, and got on the road. After a great deal of circumlocutory journeying, we arrived in Liverpool and took the old ferry to the North Wall.

All night we stood at the tiny hatch, drinking bottles of stout. When we were both exhausted, he suggested we climb into the car deck and find a warm bed. This we did and, after a lot of kissing, we crashed out soundly. We had breakfast near Bus Áras and went to the pictures to sleep it off.

As we had nowhere to stay that night, Finton suggested that we break into an empty flat. At the top of Ely Place, there was a lane and, after casing the place, we found an empty flat. Ray Cortez, the broken-down junkie had escorted us there, and since he fancied me, he didn't like the way things were shaping up. However, I was shoved through a side window into the toilet and went round to let them in the front door. We found ourselves in a comfortable three-roomed apartment with a large bed and a cupboard full of wine and sherry. We drank this and ate from all the tins we found. We stayed there happily for three nights. It turned out that our friendly landlord was a flea-circus master. Fascinating diagrams on his desk and pads full of notes told that he travelled in this unusual trade. (We never discovered who the circus master was – I'm sure there were not many in Dublin! – but we didn't think it wise to enquire too deeply into his whereabouts!) This was my introduction to Finton and his underworld philosophy.

We played the pubs, that week: Davy Byrne's, the Bailey, McDaid's. I spent money as though I had access to the Mint. As far as I was concerned, the future belonged to other people; it had nothing to do with me.

But I had to return to my children. After a week, I took the boat back, but Finton didn't want to leave. He would mosey around, he said, and maybe go back to London at some stage.

My traumatic parting with Oscar might not have existed. I had turned a page and had shifted from literature to pulp fiction.

Back in Carleton Road, with a new influx of hangers-on, I pined for Finton. When he wrote to say he couldn't afford to come back to London, I sent him the money. There is no accounting for the folly of the human heart.

All this made no difference to the parties and the excursions to Soho. The flat was full of people. Eventually Mick decided that Anna should live with him and his new family. He thought the atmosphere in the flat was dangerous for a young girl. She was turning into a lovely, independent girl who made friends easily. In the flat downstairs, there was a girl of a similar age, with whom she often played. Anna was a gifted student, and easily passed her eleven-plus. But living in the flat, with so many unfamiliar people coming and going, wasn't much fun for either of the twins, although it was easier for Jacky, because with Brian still there, she at least had a measure of security. Looking back on it, I regret giving up Anna more and more because, although I had brought up the twins till they were twelve, we missed out on each other during her adolescent years, when our friendship might have been cemented. But of course from a practical point of view, Mick was right: the place, like myself, was a mess.

Jacky, who spent all day dancing in front of the mirror, glimpsed a picture of the Ballet Rambert in a newspaper. 'That's where I want to go,' she said. So every Saturday I took her to the studio for lessons.

They were very different, my two girls. When Anna was small I used to read to her, and in this way she learned to read before she went to school. At home, she quietly amused herself, while the others needed more attention. Whereas Jacky was into physical movement and, remembering what she'd learned at the studio, would happily practise for hours, as I said, in front of the mirror. Although when she went to school, she also quickly learned to read. Billy was less of an extrovert than his two sisters, although he got on well with one of the boys upstairs.

Billy was inclined to depend on Anna's attentions at school and was upset when she left and he had to go to Holloway Secondary. Apparently he was only a few marks away from getting the eleven-plus, but they didn't let him through. He certainly had as much potential as she did, but it took time for him to develop.

So Anna went to live with Mick and, with her new stepmother Mary, would experience – I hoped – a proper family life.

*

Round about then, the Cronins moved out to a cottage in Surrey which had once been rented by George Barker. Finton and I, and Billy and Jacky, made many trips in breaking-down vehicles to stay with them. Finton began to treat me in a peculiar manner. Possibly lacking confidence amongst these illustrious people, he adopted an arrogant and swashbuckling mien. And what he lacked in confidence he made up for by treating me with masculine authority, bordering on cruelty. Even his own friends questioned this.

These outings to the Cronins were unwise. Tony was always working against the clock: one reason he wanted to get away to the country was to finish a book and some poems he was working on. These visits were, I am sure, an intrusion the Cronins could have done without.

The cottage was miles from the nearest pub, but we trailed there every evening with the children, having to drink outside in the cold because of them. One very bad night, I got a broken rib after a beating from Finton. Unable to get up the following morning, a Sunday, they went off to the pub without me. In pain, I lay in bed reading the nearest book: *Gray's Anatomy*, ironically, left there by George Barker. I began to hear noises coming from upstairs: trundlings, as though furniture was being thrown around. It was a timbered house, and I tried to reassure myself that I was listening to the wood expanding and contracting. Then the stairs began to creak, the noise getting louder and louder. Terrified, I ran barefoot out of the house and down the field.

I was cold and parched. It was drizzling, the rain slanting across the field. I tucked myself against the trunk of an oak tree, awaiting the others' return.

An hour passed. I thought I'd better make myself useful, so I went into a copse behind the house to gather wood for the fire.

229

Sooner or later, I must go back in, assert my authority over whatever malign spirit was lurking there, or convince myself that it had all been a figment of my imagination, a psychological reaction to what had happened the night before.

I went into the kitchen and was about to fill the kettle to make tea when I was again surrounded. The noises came at me from all sides, footsteps ran up and down the staircase, the house seemed to breathe and groan. Dropping the half-filled kettle, I ran out again. I ran far into the wood, my chest constricted, the rib aching, my face swollen, and huddled there until I heard their voices and laughter, and the door of the cottage opening and closing quietly.

I crept back, hangdog, apologetic for not having lit the fire. The activity in the cottage had subsided. All was quiet, as though nothing had happened. I told them of my experience. Therese said that she had sometimes heard sounds but assumed they came from the ancient timbers. She described nothing nearly as loud as what I had heard.

There is no doubt in my mind that I encountered an evil spirit that day. Or if not evil, at least one that did not want me there. Later I told George Barker about it, and he said: 'Oh yes, of course the place is haunted.' That's why he and his girlfriend had left the place.

Although I knew that George exulted in drama, he and his girlfriend had spent a volcanic time there. I came to the conclusion that this sort of conduct didn't please the spirits and that the previous night's emotional chaos had left its own particular electrical stamp, which had resulted in the poltergeist-like happenings I had experienced.

The Cronins moved out shortly afterwards and went to Spain. Finton suggested that we should stay in the house. I flatly refused. I knew that I could never be alone in that house again.

Oscar wanted me back. 'I can understand you want to sleep with Finton,' he said, 'but you have nothing in common.' He may have been right, but in my half-dazed state I couldn't listen to him.

Paul Potts, who had always had a soft spot for me, tried to persuade me to go back to Oscar. He called Finton a corner boy. 'Leave him,' he said. 'He's no good to you.' He was right.

That last year I spent in London, Robert McBryde was one of the few who understood. 'It is something to do with skin,' he said.

Finton treated his hangovers with care. He seldom rose before five in the afternoon. This made it possible for me to see Oscar at lunchtime. He had a new flat, near Hampstead Heath. He still spent nights in Hargravia, maintaining a semblance of married life with Maggie.

Lunch had always been one of our rituals. It consisted of cold ham, salad, and new potatoes when possible. And although there had been a gap in our meetings, he still made the same meal for us every day.

The first time I went there, I felt a pang of regret. He now kept a mouse in a slipper. A white mouse, whose tiny face emerged, twitching his whiskers. I took the mouse out of the slipper and cradled it in my hand, I let it run up my sleeve. Oscar and I gazed into each other's eyes.

'I love you,' he said. He had never said this to me before. You love and you lose. We fucked each other then, which we hadn't done for weeks. It was wrong that what we had had going for seven years was over. Seven years: the magic number. We were practically the same age, he a year older, our birthdays within a few days of each other. Both Pisceans.

I was struck then by a memory of taking my son Billy to the zoo. For a while, he had watched the black panther in his cage. Silently it had padded to and fro. The child had turned to me and said: 'It doesn't know which way.'

231

Do we all plod between our bars? Back and forth, back and forth. Stopping for a moment and then turning back. I can't answer this; all I know is that, just then, I was trapped. Trapped in this love business, not knowing how to escape.

Or, to put it more crudely, I was infatuated with Finton. Nothing mattered except my being with him. I am not proud of this, I simply state it. Everything, everyone, was sacrificed to this end.

As things begin, they surely end . . . with a whimper. I was pregnant again. I was running out of money. The party was over. Mrs Citovitch gave us notice. She wanted to sell the house.

Finton, Billy, Jacky, Brian and myself set off one spring day in two cars. We were on our way to catch the ferry. We'd been offered a cottage for free at the top of Tara Hill, outside Gorey, in County Wexford.

We left half the population in the flat. The electricity was cut off. I heard that the last to leave was the alcoholic former banker, Conor O'Millain. He huddled there with a candle and a blanket.

Exterminated angels.

Part Eleven

Ireland Again

Tara Hill – not to be confused with the seat of the high kings – is a rocky tor jutting out over the sea, six miles from Gorey town. It is a windswept, abandoned place. When we were there, it was dotted with a few weekend cottages, shuttered and deserted, which gave the impression of futility: the futility of the urban idea that the answer to 'getting away from it all' is to build a house – or buy an existing hovel – in such a place. Nevertheless, on 1 May 1960, after a surreal journey of squabbles and breakdowns, we landed up a boreen on Tara Hill to move into a two-and-a-half-roomed cottage with no electricity or water. There we said goodbye to Brian, who had so patiently put up with my vagaries and cruelties. Yet he showed no hostility even towards Finton, intending always to be there for Jacky. And thus he returned to London. The ring had tightened.

How was Finton supposed to behave? Remember, he was with a woman who was pregnant with his child. And in some undefined way, she seemed to be losing her attraction for him. It was no fun for him in this bleak spot, and the weather was lousy. So he decided to take the car and go to Dublin.

Abandoned in this inhospitable scree of bog and heather, I had to sort out my children. There was a Protestant national school a few miles away, so I went to see the local clergyman. He was anything but friendly. I knew that he guessed I was without a husband. 'Unwholesome' was a word I had often heard as a child, and I could read that word in his mind. I would be an unwelcome – not to mention unwholesome – member of his parish. Our meeting was brief. So I sent Bill and Jacky to the local Catholic national school, the other side of the hill.

Messages had to be fetched from Gorey on the bicycle. I skidded and slid on the boulders on the way down, with a slaughtering journey on the way back with the groceries.

The fire smoked till our eyes watered. Drinking water was away down the hill, and there was no one to talk to except the two children, who'd soon found local friends.

In a few weeks, Finton returned, but not alone. He was with Harden Rodgers, then a beautiful young student and daughter of the Belfast poet Bertie Rodgers, and John Jay, a young Dublin solicitor.

They walked along the shore below the cottage – a cold summer's day – their feet shuffling through the damp grey sand. Harden put a pebble in her mouth. 'They do this in the desert,' she said, 'to keep thirst away.' This was sophistication very different from the kind of thing those people I had left behind in London might have said. Like the child I once was, I began to listen. I trailed along behind them, trying to understand. I wanted them to play with me, but they were too busy.

'Play with me, please play with me.' Paloma turns on her. 'Stop following me.'

The next day, John and Harden went back to Dublin.

Returning to Ireland after a long time away is more traumatic than one expects. Wrapped up in the pleasant anonymity of London, one could be happily Irish, putting up with the occasional racial insult, so long as the auld sod stayed tucked away in the back of the mind, like a romantic relic. And there was the ever-present, corrosive problem of how and when to admit to one's relations, especially one's father, that one has returned to

Ireland to live. The house I had grown up in was gone, and with it my room. From now on, I would be a guest – and possibly an unwanted one at that. The returned exile is faced with almost unmanageable ambiguities. For one thing, one wants to be 'home', but one has to rediscover what it is like to live in this country called 'home', which once nearly destroyed one, yet without which life has no anchor. For a woman, reality meant hostile stares in a small community. Living with a man! Unmarried!

All the old words came tumbling back. 'Besom!' 'Strap!' 'Hussy!' There was still no shift from the old bigotry, the prying eyes, 'the Valley of Squinting Windows'.

Yet there was no going back. Most surely, the boats had been burnt.

DUBLIN ODYSSEY

There seemed no point in trying to survive in these inhospitable surroundings. So once again we packed our goods and chattels and, late one afternoon, set off.

Another horrendous journey. The car stalling, the lights failing. Eventually limping along behind a lorry.

We were given houseroom by Bob and Sheila Bradshaw in Strand Road, Sandymount. But before this, Mick Bardwell, now remarried, wrote that he wanted Billy to finish his education in England.

Billy had hated his secondary-modern school in Holloway, so I wrote back: 'Why can't he stay in Ireland? An Irish school might suit him better. I'd like him to grow up here. After all, he was born here.'

But Mick knew that there was little or no free secondary education in Ireland, and in his next letter he asked me how I would pay for his schooling. I wrote back that I'd find a way.

Strangely, Billy and Finton had begun to get on well. They'd go fishing in the local stream with bits of string and bait. I really did think that he'd be better off in this less tortured atmosphere. But Mick wouldn't listen. We went over to England and continued to argue the case. He kept saying that my arguments were specious, that he knew I'd never change. My notions of starting a new family life with Finton, as I'd told him, baking bread and being a real housewife, were as far from reality now as they had been all those years ago, when Mick and I had started out on a similar crusade. And where had that got me? He said he knew damn well that my fantasies always ended in tears. His logic was irrefutable.

While in London, I rang Oscar. A desperate ploy. A need for an ally, perhaps. We met, and a sad meeting it was. Noticing that I was pregnant, he said that he'd always wanted me to have his child.

'You never said.'

'You never asked.'

Caught once again in an ever-decreasing circle, I walked away from him.

'There are no more emotional heights to climb up or to slide down from,' I said, with a hopeless laugh.

So Billy stayed on with Mick, and Billy, as with Anna, came to look on me as a sort of second mother, to be visited sporadically throughout their teenage years.

But it was no good pretending that I had been a good mother to the twins, especially during what I call the Soho years. I had so wanted never to repeat my mother's treatment of myself and had been determined that my children would want for nothing: I had breastfed them, housed them, clothed them and found them schools – but it wasn't enough. The reason is plain for all to see: I had just handed my emotional baggage over to them and selfishly went about my business. Like the alchemist, I really believed that I would eventually turn base metal into gold, which would shine for me alone.

In a kind of a way, I suppose, this is what eventually happened – albeit many years later. Though not, as I had once hoped, through some 'gallant' arriving on his white horse to carry me away – and if not gold then at least a valuable metal gained through my novels, my poems and all my various writings, and all the hard work and friendships that went with the writing life. It was not much of an ultima Thule – how can one ever be satisfied with one's own work? – but was certainly better than nothing.

So then, with no choice but to return to Ireland, I took the ferry home once more with Jacky and the unborn baby. Gorey now abandoned, we settled into Strand Road in Sandymount.

The Cronins had introduced us to the Bradshaws, and the latter had kindly taken pity on us in our waterless hole. Bob Bradshaw, a builder by trade, was a player of the bohemian pubs, a popular man, with a rake of songs. His wife, Sheila, was one of the first to make and market Celtic-patterned jumpers in a professional way.

Compared with Tara Hill, we lived in luxury in Sandymount. There was a gas ring, electricity, and at the top of the house a large room divided in two by a screen. But money was scarce, and the loss of the few shillings the Bradshaws charged for the room made little difference.

Far as this was from pot ovens and bread baking, I still clung on to the notion of family life with Finton. But he was restless, and came and went. He was not in the least bit enamoured by the 'roses-round-the-door' ethic but was nevertheless happy to be near the city and to be able to take advantage of my dwindling fortune, renewing old friendships and starting new ones.

Jacky was sent to the local national school, and on 30 November 1960 I went into Holles Street to have my baby, Nicholas. We stayed on in Strand Road with nappies and wet bedclothes, Jacky in the corner in her bed, Finton and myself against the fireplace in our bed, the baby in his carrycot: a drawer lined with blanket. Every morning, the baby under one arm, I waded through this forest of clothes, saucepans, dishes and the previous day's rubbish to fetch a dry nappy, which was hanging over the cooker. Then I'd suckle Nicholas and try to get some order into the room – not to mention into my head!

Finton didn't tell me where he went in town: sometimes he was with John and Harden, or with some friends of John's – Bob and Nancy, an American couple who lived on Pembroke Street – and sometimes he'd strike up with an old girlfriend. He didn't tell me because he knew there'd be ructions if he did. He considered it no business of mine anyway. When I nagged him – which, of course, I did – he did what he thought most sensible men do in such circumstances: he shut me up. When my two front teeth got knocked askew, he told me to tell the dental hospital I'd fallen off my bike. In those days, if a woman got knocked about it was seen as being her own fault.

The Bradshaws seemed to turn a blind eye to all this, but it soon was made clear to us that they needed their space. Another move. This was to a flat in Upper Mount Street, belonging to an elderly lady, a friend of Connor O'Millain. Everyone called her Auntie Vi.

She charged us a pound a week for a double bed, a chaise longue for Jacky and a space on the floor for the baby. All this in Auntie Vi's own room. She slept in her single bed beside us. There was a corridor and two rooms on the return: one a kitchen, the other a damp and dark space beyond the toilet.

Patrick Kavanagh, as usual homeless, got wind of this glitzy habitat and moved into the return room, putting up with the fungoid smells.

Patrick got on well with Auntie Vi. They both loved the horses, and every day she hobbled to the bookies on her arthritic pins. They struck up a friendship based on gambling. After his morning stint in the pub, Kavanagh would burst back in, the *Irish Times* under his arm, and he and Vi would pore over the racing page together.

They teased each other like children. When Paddy deliberately threw Vi's stick on the floor, she'd say: 'Paddy, pick that up at once.' He loved being bossed around by women. Katherine bossed him; now Vi bossed him too. He'd throw the paper on the floor and stamp on it with his enormous feet, waiting for Vi to chastise him.

This house, like many another in those days, was a known haunt of oddities, so no one paid much heed to the new arrivals: an unmarried couple, a little girl and a baby, and a poet. They didn't seem to give much trouble. The beautiful baby, Nicholas, hardly ever cried.

Amongst the mishmash of tenants upstairs was the artist Charlie Brady, as yet undiscovered – and broke. Originally from the States, he swished around in a belted mac, like the detective Columbo. Crumpled canvasses littered the hall and landing. Luckily, long before he died he was discovered and subsequently came to be acknowledged as a fine painter, individual and humorous. Another American gent, who resembled Salvador Dali, with his curled moustache and chortling mien, and who owned a junk shop in Dawson Street, came home every night tipsy, and flung around the bikes that were parked in the hall.

Yet another new school had to be found for Jacky. There was a small Protestant national school in Lower Mount Street. She settled in there with a plethora of little girls who called for her every day.

The poor Prods from Ringsend kept this school going. Interesting people, who claimed that their grandparents still remembered the wild deer that would wander down to the slob lands beyond the docks. The same poor Protestants who peopled Sean O'Casey's *Water Under the Bridges*. How did they manage to escape the eagle eye of the Catholic hierarchy? They must have been a thorn in McQuaid's side!

On school outings, the mothers used to laugh at the statues in people's houses. 'Would ye look, would ye look!' – as they picked out the Virgin or a crucifix hanging in a window. They were quick for the odd pint on these outings, and one mother told me she had a grown-up son. 'Such a good boy. Never bothers with the women, takes his drinks in Bartley Dunne's.' (A well-known gay haunt in those days.)

Finton almost began to take his fatherhood seriously. Not that this ran to babysitting. Sometimes John and Harden called, so Vi babysat, and I'd be free to go with them to pubs to play bar billiards. No doubt Vi would have liked to be asked to join us, but we needed a babysitter and she got on well with Nicholas.

Up till the legs gave out, Vi had been quite a gal in the local bars in Baggot Street. Kavanagh brought her the odd Baby Power to remind her of the good times. She appeared never to have been married, and we never quite discovered what her relationship with Connor had been. They must at least have shared the same room, if not the same bed.

Although well into her sixties, she had the coiffure of a young one in her twenties: short, with curls emerging at the sides. And she wore orange lipstick and a tailor-made shirt, with a kerchief tied casually round her neck.

With this turnaround in Finton's attitude, there seemed to be a possibility of a balanced family life. But! He was beginning to get the hots for Harden, and for a short time this was reciprocated.

An academic, recently back from Cambridge University, and soon to become a junior lecturer in Trinity, was a carefree change from someone who appeared to relish the role of housewife above all else. How was I supposed to rival this scholarly beauty when milk ran out of my tits in the pub and I'd have to run home to feed the baby? And he certainly relished his persona as a swashbuckling bon viveur. All the while, John did his best, tried to see that no one was left out of these excursions, but it was clear that the main friendships and understandings were between John, Harden and Finton. And now the relationship between Finton and Harden became the pivot. It was an affair of secret meetings, amorous glances.

Looking back on it, I owe a great deal to the memory of John. (Unfortunately, he died prematurely, in the eighties.) He supported me in the bleakest of circumstances and followed my literary career assiduously. He took people to see a comedy of mine, *Thursday*, a wild romp of a play that went on in Trinity Players Theatre in the early seventies at least three times.

Finton and Harden were a strange couple all round. People took sides. There were those who couldn't stand him and supported Harden, and vice versa. John was tall, handsome, heavily built, not particularly Jewish-looking, although both his parents were Sephardic Jews. He was also generous with legal help whenever it was needed.

So John, if he minded Harden's mini-affair with Finton, didn't show it. He knew he would marry her. She would never settle for this debonair playboy. But for me, with a baby, a new pregnancy, and Jacky at national school, all of this was too much for me to carry alone.

Yes, the snake of jeolousy hissed. I was unable to stop screaming my suspicions at Finton, who would coldly turn his back on me and leave the flat.

Here was the dilemma: with the remains of my inheritance still intact, if rapidly running out, I had attracted this man, six years younger than I was, with my energy and my seemingly literary coterie, yes, but most of all with my money. The fact that the people with whom I had hung around had all been living on the edge of poverty meant that I appeared exaggeratedly well off to everyone. The rich Prod amongst the poor downtrodden Catholics. Ridiculous, in retrospect.

So why should Finton have been expected suddenly to become a good husband and wage earner when, with his undeniable charm, there were young women aplenty, with no ties or expectations, to choose from.

Regardless of all this, we muddled on for a bit till Connor wrote. He'd got a job as a chef with British Rail. He might make a flying visit.

Then there was more news. He'd thrown himself under a train as it had entered Liverpool Street Station. Having once been a respected member of society, he had been seduced by alcoholic bohemia. A slippery slope. It was a sad end.

In deep shock, Vi took a heart attack and went to hospital. We had to move again. Out came the begging bowl. John persuaded his two American friends, Bob and Nancy, to give us houseroom in Pembroke Street.

The couple kept two Alsatians, who shat on the carpet and distributed their fleas. So the flat, which had once been quite upmarket, was deteriorating rapidly. Bob and Nancy didn't hit it off, either, and they probably hoped that a third party would be some sort of buffer in their marital wars. But shortly afterwards, their world turned upside down. Nancy's new baby died. A devastating, inexplicable cot death. No one could handle this. The parents were naturally prostrated – Bob filled with guilt because he was in McDaid's when he got the phone call – had to pull themselves together for the questioning by the guards and the doctor. I felt that I was hopelessly inadequate when it came to trying to comfort Nancy, whom I barely knew. John Jay, always wonderful in an emergency or human tragedy, was their greatest support. He sorted the legal end of it, and the poor mite was buried as quickly as possible. Bob and Nancy went back to America, and we had no choice but to stay on in the flat till the lease ran out.

Absorbed as Finton was with his affairs, he was seldom at home. So as far as solving our accommodation problems went, he didn't consider it his business. He didn't mind being dragged over half of Ireland (as he put it), so long as I did the dirty work and left him in peace. But somehow or other, we had to find a place to live more permanently. We couldn't keep relying on friends or acquaintances to come to our rescue.

In the Bailey one day, I met a Mrs Noone, a fashionable lady with a black patch over one eye. She had just left her basement flat in Lower Leeson Street and was prepared to hand it over to us. We moved in.

Now, via Pembroke Street, where the fleas had danced in the sunbeams like hayseed, we landed up in this basement flat at 33 Lower Leeson Street. Two doors up, in No. 35, was the Jesuit residence where my father, Pat Hone, had been born. Riches to rags, with the tarnished-silver spoon. It seemed like moons ago when Oscar, who had stolen my christening spoon, used to take it out sometimes and kiss it.

33 Lower Leeson Street

In this deep Georgian basement, the main room, stone-floored and gritty, went the whole width of the flat. It ended in a gas fire with powdered burners. The entrance, a blackened porch, contained a leaking sink and a greasy gas cooker. Had I finally taken leave of my senses? Had Robert McBryde been right: was it really something to do with skin?

Yet we moved into this dungeon, willy-nilly: Jacky, a baby, an unborn baby, myself and Finton. And a dungeon it was. A friendly writer who knew me then remarked recently, on seeing my grown-up, successful sons, that they had all been reared in a coal-hole.

Beyond this front room, there was a corridor, off which was a series of cellars – some without light, others with a window the size of a tea tray. The farthest room faced out on to a small yard, beyond which was the toilet. As in every dungeon, the walls wept, but at least we were independent and needed to answer to no one. For this vegetal apartment, we paid £2 a week to the landlord, who lived (no doubt in a mansion) in Dublin 4.

This handsome, blond man, in a green tweed suit, arrived the day after we moved in. Rich angry men are different from penurious ones, and they never frighten me. By and large, they are bastards and not worth thinking about. He was clean, and very angry.

'You never told me you had children,' he barked.

'I never told you I hadn't,' I snapped, standing at the door.

In holy Ireland, where the family is the be-all and end-all of society, there are few landlords who will let you a flat if you have children. In their eyes, a child is a bomb that will raze their property to the ground as soon as the door is opened. And of course they are afraid that they won't get you out when they want to sell.

This gentleman was no different. His own children had nannies and au pair girls and nurseries with padded walls, no doubt, but my children were bound to destroy his valuable piece of property overnight. A week later, he had his solicitor draw up an agreement that I would act as caretaker for the property and would vacate the premises when I was asked to do so, with no notice period. This was a loophole that his cunning lawyer had ferreted out. In fact, we stayed there for nine years.

By now I was nearly destroyed with guilt for not having informed my father of my whereabouts. I knew that this situation could not go on much longer: Ireland is notoriously small, and sooner or later he would hear through the grapevine that I was in the country, and then there'd be hell to pay. Even before I was married, he had stated quite clearly that he didn't care what I did so long as I didn't do it at home. So I'd have to steel myself to admit to having been in Ireland for quite some time – with a new man and another child, and a baby on the way. In other words, doing exactly what he had dreaded.

I rang his house and confessed. He was angry. My stepmother told me that I had been thoughtless, and that Pat had been very worried about my whereabouts. I found this hard to believe, but I think it was true. Or was it? Even at this distance, I think Pat's emotions in this respect were tempered by dread. Dread as to what new disgrace I'd bring on his head. Also, of course, he found it impossible to give voice to any emotion other than disapproval. This is not to say that he was a bad or cruel man, it was just that he wanted a bit of peace. And praise didn't come easily to parents in those days. I don't think he ever actually voiced his approval even of Paloma, whom he so admired for her athletic prowess. The old adage 'Spare the rod and spoil the child' was the recurring dictum with him. Even when I showed him my first book of poems, he burst out laughing, saying: 'I thought poems rhymed!'

Nobody really wanted me in Ireland. Even the junior partner in the firm of Collis and Ward who dealt with my dwindling savings tried to persuade me to return to England, arguing that, financially, I'd be much better off there. In other words, get out while you still have a few bob left.

I would embarrass them, they felt. I could be relied on to do the wrong thing at family gatherings. I might cry at funerals, or get drunk at weddings. My brother Noll dreaded my presence too, and made sure not to tell me until after the event if a relation had died.

Anyway, terrified as I was of admitting to having settled in Ireland, I made the confession, hangdog, pretending, as ever, that things were hunky-dory. And surprisingly, he took it – or at least as much as of it as I dared tell him – with comparative equanimity. He was getting on – he was well into his seventies – and was happily married, with a son about to go to college, and it's possible he felt that there was no point in his worrying about me any more. He probably looked on me as a lost cause, or at any rate beyond repair! So the result of this was that, from time to time, I brought the family out to their house for tea and stability. As it has turned out, these excursions meant a lot to the children, and as grandparents, Pat and Valerie became important to them. Unfortunately, until I acquired a banger, we had to rely on Finton to bring us out in his taxi. Often, this meant that we waited all afternoon for him to get out of bed and it was far too late when we eventually arrived. I was always so embarrassed about this but was unable to explain anything, ever. I was still as tongue-tied when with my father as I had been when I was six years old!

Yes, by now the taxi had become part of our lives. There was only one thing Finton liked doing, apart from chasing women, and that was driving. I still had £300 in the bank, so I decided that I should buy a taxi. We shopped around and found a Ford Consul. Finton got the licence from the Carriage Office and for the next four years earned enough to keep himself in drink and to give me a pound a day for the household needs.

By dint of finding the cheapest items in all the grocers in Camden Street and buying vegetables off the stalls, I managed to give the growing family a decent diet. One could buy cigarettes in ones from a huckster in Hatch Place, a lane at the back of Leeson Street. Half a crown could provide a supper. Herrings were a penny each. The best mince, a shilling a pound. Oranges, five for a shilling. It wasn't easy, but it wasn't impossible.

With my expanding belly, I trundled the broken go-cart, with Nicholas on board, round to Camden Street every day. The pound was always gone by nightfall. Naturally the responsibility of finding money for the bills and children's needs fell to me. And being of an inventive nature, I found all sorts of ways to make the few bob. I'd always made my own and my children's clothes, so now I took to making clothes to order. I'd tackle anything from Kinsale cloaks to wedding dresses! Also, of course, I made clothes for the boys, Jacky and myself. Otherwise, I reviewed books for *Hibernia*: the then editor was very good to me and gave me a book to review nearly every week. Then Jacky would sell the book in Greene's of Clare Street. 'We'll eat that,' I'd say. Another trick was to tell the children bedtime stories, write them down the next day, and sell them to the radio. We lived on the edge, all right, but at least we lived!

Nicholas hadn't liked this move: babies seldom care for upheavals, and he was no exception. So we spent as much time as possible in Stephen's Green in order to give him room to play, and fresh air. But the long nights lengthened, and winter was torture.

Finton, as a working man, expected a large meal when he got in, often two hours late, having spent the intervening time in McDaid's. If it was mincemeat or a herring, he'd say: 'What's for dinner?' And like all contemporary Irish males in those days, he really did believe that men didn't push prams. And they didn't.

On 20 March 1962, my son Edward was born. 'Strong, straightforward English names,' Finton had insisted. 'None of your namby-pamby Irishisms.' He despised the Irish, said that their backs were aching for the lash. Strangely enough, in spite of this, he spoke quite good Irish himself.

It was a tortuous labour, threatening a breach birth. The midwife turned the child round with difficulty. I hallucinated with the pains.

Like lowing cows, women crowded the labour ward. There was not enough gas and air to go round. The pains, which I now believed to be alternatively male and female, crowded my mind. I kept thinking: 'The next female pain will be the last.' The over-worked nurses ran from bed to bed, slapping faces in frustration when there were screams. There were no doctors in public wards unless you paid good money. From the moment you step inside the antenatal clinic, they call you 'mother'. You had no identity, no soul: you were simply a living means of reproduction, an iso-lated organism of no intrinsic importance. (But it must be added here that this was in the sixties. It is hoped that things are a lit-tle different now!)

When, finally, the baby came, one midwife said about some flowers John Jay had sent me: 'We'd better give them to the lady at the end of the ward.' Naturally, I thought she meant some woman even worse off than I was, but it turned out to be the Virgin Mary, to thank her for the mother and child's being alive!

In those days breastfeeding was discouraged, as a shamefully dirty habit! And it has to be admitted that this was worse in Ireland than in England: when Jacky was born in Hampstead General Hospital, there was no bother with breastfeeding. So with each child, my decision to breastfeed was looked upon with suspicion. Bad enough having no husband, but that dirty notion!

Back in Leeson Street, with a new baby, a toddler still in nappies, and Jacky. The very first minute, while my head was bent to feed the baby, Finton went out the door and disappeared. He wasn't going to waste any more time on domesticity. The three days I'd been in Holles Street had been an absurd importunity on a man of his sensitivity and calibre. It turned out that it was Jacky who had looked after Nicholas while Finton was cavorting in the west with an old girlfriend.

How could I have managed to get through those years without Jacky? She cleaned and scrubbed the old frayed carpet. She took the babies out in their prams, walking down the canal bank, while still only at national school. And she was great company.

More nappies, wet blankets, constant feeding. Worse still, after ten days Ed developed a post-natal allergy, a rash which covered his whole body. He had to go into the clinic across the road from the maternity hospital, and I went there every four hours to feed him. I had to run all the way to Holles Street, my breasts engorged between the feeds. But the poor mite. What else could be done?

Back home again, a bare three weeks later, he began to vomit continuously. Worried sick, I called the doctor. This nonchalant, stupid man, said: 'Put him on the bottle. Your milk's not agreeing with him.' Ignoring this rubbish, I picked Ed up that night and ran down to Harcourt Street Children's Hospital. There was hurt in his big blue eyes as he gazed up at me in the waiting room. When the intern came, he shouted: 'This baby can't stay here. He has gastroenteritis. He must go immediately to the Fever Hospital in Cherry Orchard.'

'Can I go with him?'

'Certainly not!'

I watched him being carried away in an ambulance, the doors clanging shut on the tiny mite.

The following day, Nicholas and I took the bus to the hospital. There he was, tucked away behind screens, and once again no one was to be let near him. However, to give the doctors their due, their treatment was miraculous. Edward had reacted to the antibiotics immediately and was already on the mend. Two weeks later, he was home. This experience was shattering for me. What folly was it trying to create a family in this damp, dark hole? But I was caught in the poverty trap, and there seemed to be no way out.

So Ed was recovering. Perhaps because of his awful experiences, he became one of the most tractable babies ever known. He'd lie happily in his pram playing with his car, making zooming noises far in advance of his years. And at six months, he said his first word: 'Car!'

So life continued in this triple-edged fashion.

The Salon!

When one is exhausted physically, one becomes a sort of automaton. And in a certain way, it seemed that only half of me took part in these almost-nightly gatherings, maybe getting a second wind after a couple of swigs of beer. But in many ways I am lucky. I don't suffer from depression, and although I may be afraid of heights and a touch paranoid – imagining that shop-keepers think me some kind of freak – I have an abundance of extra energy which I can put into overdrive. And just as the law has loopholes if you look carefully, so has life. I began to write again.

I had begun in London, secretly writing poems and short stories, but had been terrified to show them to anyone. So now, on top of having babies – which one might think was enough to occupy oneself with – I got stuck into the typewriter. As I said, I had been reviewing books and selling the occasional talk or children's story to RTÉ since 1960. But now the poems started coming. I began to get more confidence, partly because friends had started to gather round me, and they were extraordinarily supportive.

So while the children crawled around on the floor, I typed away on my ancient machine. Poem after poem, some of them terrible, no doubt, but the friends who gathered were patient enough to read them. They came from McDaid's, when the pub was closed; they came from the Bailey. John Jordan, still lecturing in UCD, arrived with a coterie of his own admirers, mostly students in their final year. Dicky Riordan, then a medical student, the poets Macdara Woods, Paul Durcan, Brian Lynch and Michael Hartnett (low-sized, wiry, like an anxiety-ridden monkey) – all of whose extraordinary talents were already manifesting themselves – and many others. Every morning, there were new poems to read, trickling in from all sides.

Homeless people came and settled like plovers. Bene Ryan moved in behind the screen. The flat contracted into cubicles. One of the cellars had a half-door; I called this 'the Horsebox'. It was a cavernous room with no light, but someone could sleep there when they were stuck.

Friends came after-hours with the bottle of whiskey and the bottles of stout. On the wind-up gramophone, inherited from the landlord, they played 'Wrap the Green Flag Round Me, Boys', 'Linden Lea' ('poem by Barnes, music by Vaughan Williams', John always said with a chuckle). And John would sing in his cracked alto:

> Hello young lovers, wherever you are.
> Don't cry because I'm alone.
> All my good wishes go with you tonight,
> I've had a love of my own.
> I know how it feels to have wings on your heels
> And to walk down the street in a trance.
> And to walk down the street
> On the chance that you'll meet,
> And you'll meet not merely by chance.

Mock-mournful when it ended. And there were plenty of other old seventy-eights lying around, from John McCormacks to popular ditties. 'Girl of a million dreams, when will my dreaming come true . . . .'

The parties grew louder and louder. There was violence. Blood, booze and songs! And shiners! Very slippery, the outside world!

Finton, although always there, reacted oddly to these gatherings. He didn't care to see these new admirers clustering round – mostly attractive young men.

I use the epithet 'salon' with some irony. These gatherings were far from the kind of salon that was once known of in the time of Louis XIV, or indeed the ones in which Æ or Yeats participated fifty years previously, yet it became a place for these young poets to discuss their work and escape from the pressures of home. It makes me laugh to think of myself as a patron: the poor visitors never got a scrap to eat, and John Jordan – the only one of us with a steady income – paid for all the drink. In fact, in a strange way I felt invisible half the time. I detested also the notion of being thought an eccentric character. I really did believe in my work, and in my apprenticeship as a poet. Since the age of six, writing had been not an ambition but a *condition*. Something one is born with, like a hunchback or having one leg shorter than the other.

Since these young people came uninvited – although they were welcome – I felt that it was nothing to do with me personally. As a result, it seemed odd that Finton was so antagonistic towards the gatherings. I suppose that like all men in those days, he hated the notion of having a writer as a partner. And this led to a number of very nasty encounters, with his mixed-up feelings of being the emotional boss while taking a sideline in the literary stakes.

One afternoon, a poet was visiting from England. Finton happened to come in, and found us chatting on the sofa. This was more than he could stand. He picked up the chopper, terrifying the Englishman, who ran from the flat. I ducked and crawled, trying to hide – under the table, under the chairs, anywhere. I knew I was in real danger.

Yet something must have held him back. I supposed he believed that there was only one way to keep a woman in line, and that was not necessarily to kill her but to warn her that he was serious and would always be the boss.

And of course, lies had to be told to the hospital staff. In a story I wrote and published years later called 'Outpatients', I dealt humorously with the reaction of the nurses.

Whenever I sent out stories of family violence to David Marcus, they were rejected. Not until the eighties were the citizens of holy Ireland allowed to read such calumny. Poor men! Did their lives have to be ruled by a nagging scald?

Roddy Doyle's novel *The Woman Who Walked Into Doors*, published in 1996, is one of the few books that deal with this subject subtly. It shows how a woman caught in this trap blames herself. The book outraged many strong feminists, who couldn't understand why the woman in the novel didn't leave her husband. But of course, things are rarely as simple as that!

With all the racket, people believed there were orgies going on in the basement, though nothing could have been further from the truth. These parties were asexual – a bit wild, maybe, and funny. But gossip was rife: the tenants upstairs complained to the landlord. Letters passed between them. We had only one ally, Miss White, a straggly-grey-haired old lady with a liking for the drop, and for whom messages in Dwyer's pub were done most nights – a Baby Powers and a half-bottle of port. She was one of the few people who realised that Finton was not entirely to blame for his actions. She said: 'You spoil him and then you nag at him. What do you expect?' She, rightly, did not have much sympathy for this particular victim!

So the sixties in Leeson Street were a mass of contradictions. On the one hand, there was a man with excessive emotional power who knew exactly how to humiliate the woman he lived with. She, on the other hand, was a serious housewife and mother who doled out the money so that the children got decent meals and a modicum of care. The third aspect of it was that she was the centre of what would later become the cream of literary Dublin – Durcan, Woods, Hartnett, and later Eiléan Ní Chuilleanáin – while she was cutting her teeth at the feet of the likes of Kavanagh and John Jordan.

Yet the children were my anchor. I was overly fussy about feeding them properly, never allowing them tatty food. I fussed over how much protein and fresh vegetables and fruit they got – possibly to the detriment of their appearance, about which I was too casual. But of course, in many ways I resented my lack of freedom: all my visitors who were childless could come and go at any time of day.

One of my main difficulties was that there were no neighbouring children around – no other families with whom my children could play. Only for a short while in the mid-sixties was I lucky enough to meet the Higginses – Aiden and his wife Jill – who had two sons much the same age as mine. Jill and I became friends and almost every other day I'd bring my boys over to their flat in Ranelagh – and the kids would play happily together. Also, when I acquired a car, I'd take them picnicking in Wicklow. But the sad thing was that, shortly afterwards, the Higgins family took off to Spain. So once more I had to put up without any outside support or diversions for my sons.

Looking back on it, though, I like to think that in some strange way the children fitted in with the madness. There were hilarious incidents. On one occasion, Nicholas, with an impish smile, ran to the cooker and turned on all the gas burners without lighting them, then ran out, as if to say: 'That'll get rid of you.' Kavanagh, who had moved in, forever afterwards beamed over the memory, constantly repeating: 'He turned on the gas! He turned on the gas!'

Kavanagh took an interest in the children. He often said that he wondered how they would turn out, with all these writers around them. Would they subconsciously absorb the wisdom and humour with which they were surrounded? Whether because of this or not, the three boys all turned out to be in one way or another extremely talented.

On another occasion, Nick found a half-full bottle of cider in the cupboard and kept running in and out of the living room, taking swigs from it. He was quite soon drunk, and took off his clothes, racing round like a dervish. Unfortunately, he fell on the concrete and scored his back. He had to be rushed to Vincent's Hospital to get his back sprayed – with me hoping that the nurse wouldn't smell his breath! Bad enough having a mother who takes a drink, but a drunken child! Curtains to a family. Ed's endearing qualities included a taste for pyromania. He once set the curtains by the fireplace ablaze. But all this devilment was more in fun than anger and ultimately came to no harm.

It was nothing short of a miracle that the children survived in this heady atmosphere, living as they were in a dingy hole, with little money and unreliable parents. Maybe it was serendipity!

GETTING PUBLISHED

James Liddy, recently returned from the States, decided to start a poetry magazine, *Arena*. He read my poems and wanted to publish some of them. So more and more poems came tumbling out. One after the other, like sheep going through a gap. This was the beginning of a long haul. A bumpy journey, full of hazards and potholes, which, of course, can only end with death. Thus getting my first work published was largely due to the luck of meeting Liddy, and also Kavanagh, John Jordan and the young poets.

The establishment of *Arena* was a real milestone in Dublin, as there was nothing of that nature going on at the time. In fact, there was very little outlet of any kind for literary activity. (Poetry Ireland had folded some years before.) So those who got their first poems published by James were much indebted to his enthusiasm and perspicacity.

JOHN JORDAN

John never wanted to leave the parties, and sometimes he'd sit up all night reading a detective novel. And if it was a Sunday morning, he'd wait till the various Masses were over so that his mother would assume that he'd been to church.

He was one of those thin, angular men whom I thought resembled the caterpillar in *Alice in Wonderland*. He always sat sideways, frame bent, his long legs roped round each other. He had a long, pulpy face with a lopsided smile. When he was amused, he'd say: 'Oh my dear! Oh my dear!'

A classical scholar, he'd frittered away his Oxford scholarship, while enjoying his friendship with the notorious Enid Starkie. Yes, a scholar of a high calibre. His memory was prodigious. Any literary reference could be underscored by John if you made a mistake.

In spite of missing some of his lectures, he was still on the staff of UCD, and many students said that he was one of the most exhilarating lecturers they'd ever had. Eventually he got an early-retirement grant because of 'ill health.' This kept him on a subsistence level thereafter. However, his health did not really deteriorate until the mid-eighties. He continued his scholarly activities, reviewing and writing essays, and composing stories of his own – and a lot of quirky poetry. He published a good few collections of poems but, unfortunately, his collected stories weren't published till after his death.

He was one of those people whom fate decrees will never be happy with his achievements. Someone who is in the dilemma of having a scholarly mind yet longs to be recognised for his own particular talent. His stories are very moving, very funny, his tenderness towards young men manifest. Yet when they were finally published, they received minimal attention.

He used to give me a few bob for typing his stories. One day, when delivering a typescript to his house, I had the temerity to ask his mother did her husband drink. (Mrs Jordan had been a widow for many years, her husband having been a cooper in Guinness's.) She said in answer: 'He would take the odd bottle of stout, not like Jack here. But then, of course, Jack's a genius.'

They had an extraordinary relationship. They knew 'the script' off by heart.

'I'm going out with Mrs Bardell.' (John's nickname for me.)

'No you're not.'

'Yes I am.'

'No you're not. Finish up the story you're writing.'

'I will not. Where are my socks?'

'Wherever you put them.'

But he always won. On his way out, he called back from the hall, where a picture of the pope hung: 'Your Pole is crooked!'

There's no doubt that they adored each other, and she worried about him night and day. He had had TB and was never strong. In his later years, alcohol was his only solace.

One can only go halfway to describing John, his sense of humour, his scholarship, his many kindnesses. There is no doubt that he had a stake in the big bad world of literature. But of such an individual nature, it is likely that only the most assiduous reader will mine him out of oblivion. But this surely will happen one day. In fact, the young writer Eamonn Sweeney mentioned his stories as forgotten gems only recently.

But who remembers John as a person now? Only a few loyal friends. The then young medical student Dickie Riordan was one of his staunchest companions in those early days, with his keen intelligence and scatty humour. They were perfect companions as they roamed the streets at night.

In his later years, John would spend lonely hours in Grogan's, having begun the day with a triple vodka, thereafter staying on, sadly silenced, brightening up occasionally when an old friend chanced to call in. He needed intellectual stimulus badly. He was lonely and frustrated when all his friends had split up or were busy living their own lives. When his *Collected Poems* were published posthumously, Macdara Woods wrote a magnificent introduction, which goes a long way towards redressing the balance.

The novelist and poet Dermot Healy has a lasting memory of John in Annamakerrig. Each night over a bottle of spirits, their intellects sparked off each other. But this was now rare. More often, he seemed to be preoccupied with some distant mystery, his 'mammy' being his only anchor.

When he died in the late eighties, as is always the case in Ireland, they came from far and wide. Hucksters and poets, barmen and lawyers. It was the last of the great bohemian funerals. Poems were read and songs were sung far into the night.

Some years before this, he had written a laudatory review of my stories and poems. I was lucky to have known him in his more halcyon days.

PREGNANT AGAIN

Nineteen sixty-three. I found myself pregnant again.

Finton had been going through various affairs. He called a pretty girl 'a blonde' as though there were no other hair colours. Two aristocratic 'blondes' had moved into a flat across the road. One of them a Leslie, the other a Dunsany. This was heady stuff!

Leonie Leslie, a swashbuckling twenty-odd-year-old, had the edge on the young Dunsany, but having the daughter of a lord over the way, Finton went through the snobbish routine – not unmindful of Mary Hone's pathetic attempts to climb the aristocratic ladder. But Finton was no arse-licker, and they enjoyed his villainous attentions. The result was that he spent all his free time in their flat.

It was hard to match up to these sirens. When Paul Durcan happened to call one afternoon, I persuaded him to accompany me across the road. I picked up a bin-lid on the way. At the foot of the steps leading up to their flat – it was a sort of maisonette – was a front door with a large glass panel. I hurled the bin-lid at the glass, which shattered into a million pieces.

'You'll pay for this!'

'What with?'

Such were the goings and comings in No. 33, as it came to be known in the early 1960s. Nothing was planned. It was like a concatenation of events, each one jammed into the next. But the

264

kernel, of course, was the writing. Poems being inspected, ruled on, criticised, edited. There was rapport amongst the writers – affection, even.

I've tried to give a worm's-eye view of those years – of the people who passed through, their loyalty, their hilarity. There were excursions to Limerick and other places to give readings, with absurd incidences – like begging for money while the organisers hid under their desks.

But to go back to my personal situation. It's not easy to describe that year of my pregnancy, cursed with poverty, emotional insecurity and fatigue.

That same year, my Aunt Olive had died. The same aunt who had supported me and believed in me, throughout my childhood, had cut me out of her will for many reasons. For being a communist, a non-practising Protestant, divorced, and living in sin – to name but a few. I had looked forward to some money from her, and getting none was a profound shock.

From time to time, I had made an effort to drag at the reins of our one-time relationship and take the children out to her house, but my aunt was very old, her past too far away, and she had spent the last twenty years lavishing her affections on Paloma's children, Gail and Anne.

On my very last visit to my aunt, I told her: 'You were very good to me as a child.'

'Was I?' the old lady asked, surprised.

Now, the aunt's lovely house on the Malahide Road was to be sold, Gail being the sole occupant. So partly out of revenge, and partly to get away from the coal-hole, I took Nick and Eddy (Jacky being on holiday with her father) out to stay there.

I seldom drank when I was pregnant, but this time it was more than my usual sickness: I discovered I had viral hepatitis. John Jordan tried to cheer me up with whiskey. I asked him politely to go away. 'I can't drink,' I said. The virus had been brought in by a friend, and gradually a few of us went down with it. A horrible, debilitating disease. The whites of my eyes had turned yellow. I was in a bad way.

Since Jacky was away, I had to rely on three-year-old Nicholas to do the messages. He loved running. Always, when we went to Sandymount strand, he'd disappear into the horizon, way out towards the sea, a dot speeding away, like the phenomenal athlete that he would later become. So with a note in his hand, he'd be despatched for tea or sugar, or whatever was needed. Because of his being so small, he might have to do two or three runs in order to carry the needed groceries.

So while I was still very sick, out we all went to this beautiful house. Finton, naturally, seeing another big house as his goal, came along too. Here, he proceeded to lock himself into a little room while Nicholas and I slept upstairs, with Eddy in his pram.

Eddy, at the age of one and half, had become a philosopher. Having had a tortured babyhood, he had nevertheless decided to survive. (He'd had pneumonia at six months, which had meant another stay in hospital.) So every morning, we went out on the lawn, and I'd sit at my typewriter, the two kids playing around my chair. Still jaundiced and very tired, but glad to be away from Leeson Street, I worked away at a play I was writing.

Gail was the most important person in the house. A beautiful young student, now on holidays. Both Finton and John Jay took a shine to her. Then, unfortunately, she got the virus and fell sick. They cosseted her with grapes and goodies.

As is well known, jaundice is one of the most depressing conditions. It didn't take Shakespeare to tell us that the liver is the seat of the emotions! But the play, willy-nilly, had to be worked on.

And a strange play it was. A black comedy. It was about someone who was always pregnant – not surprising – and there were no weekdays, only weekends. Saturday, Sunday, Saturday Sunday. Eventually I sent it to RTÉ, and they wrote back: 'It seems to be written in some kind of rhyme.' It's true, it was written in a species of blank verse. As I remember: iambic pen-tameters!

Then a strange event: Oscar suddenly arrived on his scooter, with his new woman, Anna. I sat on the wall in the front of this lovely house, numbed, bemused, while he kissed and hugged me, while the babies crawled around the gravel.

'Are you not pleased to see me?' he asked.

'I don't know.'

'Its just like when your twins were small and we met first,' he said.

He told me that they intended to visit the Cliffs of Moher because I used to tell him that if ever I wanted to commit sui-cide, I'd choose to throw myself over the cliffs into the swirling black waters below.

Oscar and this tall, handsome woman, with golden hair, in a black-leather suit and high-heeled boots, seemed like people who were very far away. As though it was no longer possible for me to get a purchase on the shifting sands of other people's lives.

I remembered the time I had sat on the stairs as a child in Leixlip and chewed the broken glass. But I hadn't swallowed the shards. No, I hadn't swallowed them.

'When are you going to Clare?' I asked, for something to say. I could feel the tiny pulsating movement of the foetus.

'Quite soon. We'll stay over somewhere.'

'You'll find wild mushrooms there. Don't fall off the edge.'

We all laughed.

They both got astride the bike, and I listened to the *phut-phut* as it faded away into the distance.

No, I hadn't swallowed the glass.

People came out to visit – John Jay, James Liddy and others – and were suitably impressed by this beautiful house, its sweep of lawn and herbaceous borders.

'We'll have a party,' I said. And although I wasn't drinking, I had masses of beer and spirits bought. What possessed me? Revenge again. Revenge on my aunt for forgetting me. Revenge on my bitch of a mother for hating me. The place could have been destroyed. It was like something a rich teenager would do when the parents went away. I was terrified my father would hear about it. Could I never *not* do the wrong thing?

Clearly we couldn't stay forever. The place was being put up for auction. So back we trudged to our coal-hole.

Back in No. 33, I began to practise mind over matter. 'Why can animals have their young with seemingly little pain?' I asked myself. I realised that I couldn't go through another labour as bad as the last. So it was up to me to prevent it. Going to the prenatal clinic had always been pointless, and only humiliated the mothers. I booked myself in semi-private, having no idea how I'd pay for it. I hoped that, with the help of the gas and air, the birth might be less of an ordeal. Although I used every kind of illegal contraceptive, and got pregnant as easily as a rabbit, I was the wrong shape for having babies: my pelvis was too narrow.

During those last six months of my pregnancy, Leeson Street didn't change much. I still couldn't take any alcohol, so the parties were less hectic, and from time to time John Jay bought me a lemonade in McDaid's. But the literati still came and went, Kavanagh on the long couch under the window.

In the mornings, he'd say: 'Will you mix my Complan?'

'Without lumps?'

Sometimes he made me nervous. I had an uneasy feeling he had come to disapprove of me.

He saw I was pregnant again and told me I was foolish to stay up so late. 'I know, Paddy' was all I could say.

But there was a comicality (his favourite word) about Kavanagh, no matter how sick he was. When John Jordan, never quite having thrown off the influence of his Catholic upbringing, said he thought my babies should be christened, Kavanagh broke out laughing. 'It's not as if they had the *masles*!' he said, deliberately accentuating his Monaghan accent.

The trouble was that, with all the babies and parties, I was not able to give him the attention he needed. He hankered after Katherine's care. There was a Christmas dinner when there was a last-minute purchase of a turkey. When he had been persuaded to partake of this, he muttered: 'Very *dhry*. Very *dhry*. Not like the duck Katherine cooked.'

He needed someone less preoccupied than I was to talk to in the mornings. I was always glad when Macdara came round, because he and Paddy had much in common, Macdara having spent much of his early youth in County Meath – to compare with Kavanagh's Monaghan.

It was a hard time for him. He needed to start the day with a Baby Powers, so I'd be dispatched to Dwyer's for the message. He'd ring his hands round Nicholas's face so he wouldn't cry when he saw me leaving. Nicholas didn't mind this at all. Kavanagh also liked Jacky and once offered her a pound if she'd sing 'The Minstrel Boy' with the right timing. He believed singing was all to do with timing. Hitting the right notes was important, of course, but timing was everything. Perhaps it is something to do with life! (Incidentally, he didn't pay her the pound then, but some time later she met him in Stephen's Green and said 'Hello Paddy, you owe me a pound' – and he gave it to her!)

Through all this, I continued to write poems and publish them in either *Arena* or the *Holy Door*, edited by Michael Hartnett. Kavanagh read the poems with glee. Later on in the sixties I wrote the first draft of the novel *Girl on a Bicycle*.

On 5 March 1964, John was born. And apart from Jacky's, his was the quickest and easiest birth I had had. Mind over matter!

I raced down the corridor, being chased by an official asking for money, and on out of Holles Street and up Merrion Square with the baby in my arms. Perhaps because of this athletic flight, I unfortunately started to haemorrhage as soon as I got to Leeson Street. By some fluke, Noll happened to call, and he drove the baby and me back to the hospital. Then, for some ridiculous reason, they wouldn't let me keep John with me, so he had to be taken back and weaned. This was a great pity, because he lost out on breastfeeding in those important early days after birth. Once more, Jacky took on the task. Anyone would wonder was there ever a time when I wasn't running out of a maternity hospital with a baby in my arms!

Like all my babies, however, John was a survivor. He was very beautiful and, in spite of his traumatic first weeks, had a famously infectious laugh. From early on, he showed unusual wit, and since I was always reading to the three of them books that were well ahead of their years, like the others, when he started talking his vocabulary was remarkable.

We had now acquired a 'pick-up' – a Black Box – and a heterogeneous collection of records, from Beethoven's Violin Concerto to the Clancy Brothers, and from *The Songs of Percy French*, to Mozart's Clarinet Quintet. And John, before he could walk or barely talk, would lever himself up on to the table and put on a record, and contentedly lean against the box.

Then out of the blue, Robert McBryde turned up. Homeless as usual. A few years previously, Colquhoun had died, and McBryde, penniless and lonely, had gone from house to house till he ferreted me out in Leeson Street. A screen was put up in a corner of the sitting room and a settle bed installed – an old camp bed found in the Daisy Market.

Robert fell in love with John and called him 'the Wonder Child'. That's how John got his names: 'John' after John Jordan, 'Robert' after McBryde and 'Finton' after Finton. (I liked the name!)

Ireland in the Sixties – and Finton McLachlan

While this coterie of artists and writers hung around Leeson Street, the country was going through vast changes. The era of a new freedom. Hippies and flower power and peace for all. The Beatles, Bob Dylan et al. Yet there was behind all this a great deal of unacknowledged poverty. The working classes still had no hold on things. There was no great new influx of jobs. Men drank the pitiful dole and women went out to clean – if they could find work. The Catholic hierarchy was hard put to keep the citizens in line. But the poor are easily seduced, and kept on having babies, and McQuaid managed to continue his anti-contraceptive war, convincing 90 percent of the population that women were made for God and procreation.

But certainly it was a momentary haven for the educated middle classes. If there were jobs to be got, they got them. In the professions, in the radio and television stations, in the newspapers. But for someone without a degree, those doors were closed. Only ill-paid freelancing – and lucky to get that!

There are those who still consider the sixties (the swinging sixties!) a kind of nirvana or utopia, but very many remember that time as a bleak era without a glimmer of hope for the underprivileged. The dole was negligible. Sunday suits were pawned on Mondays. Housing in the city was overcrowded and unhygienic, and the government of the time, with great moral insensitivity, imagined that it could counteract the situation by building those disastrous towers in Ballymun. I had to exert all my powers of invention to bring in extra money, but there were a great many people in my situation, without my energy or abilities, who simply could not make ends meet.

*

But back to the real conundrum. Why did I stay with this man who did his utmost to put me down? And who made cutting remarks about my appearance just as my mother had done when I was a child. Remarks such as: 'You're not going out looking like that?' – when I'd made an effort to look good. The reasons were manifold. I was too poor to make a getaway with the children. In no circumstances would I allow my father or stepmother to know I was living in these terrible circumstances, and so I would never have asked for sympathy. But the real gist of the matter was that I still imagined that there was a possibility of real family life with him. I believed that the kids should have a father, however unstable. But looking back on it, his behaviour was inexplicable. He had entered into this liaison *faute de mieux*, had fathered three sons, and in his own way possibly felt inextricably trapped. A person in this situation can only maintain his equilibrium by making sure that he is in control, so he exerted all his powers to that end. Jacky, a perspicacious child, used to say: 'Stop trying to please him. You only do it because if you don't, he makes life unbearable.'

But then there were the outings, the picnics, the excursions. When there was still the taxi – it died in the late sixties – and later an old car my Aunt Phyllis had given me, we were off to the mountains, and Lough Dan, or the Liffey basin, or Glendalough, lighting fires and camping and swimming in the lakes, nearly every weekend. How to explain this dichotomy in his personality? His face would light up as he plunged through thickets or jumped over rocks. We all loved the mountains and were sometimes able to stay overnight in my Uncle Bob's farm in Bo Island on Calary bog.

Later, when there was crowd-extra work on the films, we'd camp near the set. And when Billy or Anna were over, the whole family would take off.

Yes, big B-movies were coming in then, with vast crowd scenes. And this meant money, real money. The whole family were put on the crowd panel, and films like *The Viking Queen, Sinful Davie, A New Black Beauty* and many others brought in work for all of us. There are some wonderful shots of the three boys in *Black Beauty* – one of the many *Black Beauty* films – covered in mud, throwing clods of earth and suchlike, with blackened faces. And the boys got jobs in ads also, under the aegis of Michael Colbert and Tiernan McBride. On one occasion, Eddy came home sick from having eaten so many cream buns for the different takes!

The last film that gave us a lot of work was *Alfred the Great*. I heard that it was being filmed in Connemara, and in the ancient Mini that Eiléan had given me – the said vehicle in exchange for the wind-up gramophone – I set off with the three boys and Jacky to land up in Moycullen in County Galway, where we pitched our tent near a little stream.

I had hoped to get away without Finton – for once, to assert my independence, against his grinding need to control us – but needless to say, he followed us in his taxi. However, the next day we were at the set, hoping for work. Jacky and Finton and I were taken on – Finton really happy because he could sleep all day, since he was a dead Dane. I got about three weeks' solid work: this meant unheard-of wealth. Yet even in these circumstances, where we were able to eat three meals a day on the set, Finton had to assert his authority back in the camp. He insisted on another meal being cooked on the open fire.

But it was a wonderful summer. The sun shone, and there was poitín up the hill, which we bought and sold at a profit to the other extras. David Hemmings had been told that Irish extras were chatty and not to mind them (seemingly English crowd-extras never talk to the stars!), which didn't suit him. And when he fell into a stream, misquoting his line as 'We need some more fucking villagers', one of the cameramen had to resign. We hadn't had such fun and freedom from worry for years. I was wanted in every scene – the woman with the good face – one minute in the north of England, next minute in the south – much to the director's amusement.

When the film was over, we were lent a cottage in Kilbaha which was owned by my cousin, Patsy Cooper, where we fished lobster off the cliffs, risking the loss of the valuable pots. One midnight, our neighbour came shouting: 'Beach the bloody crates! The sea is rising.' A poem, 'Lobster Fishing', came out of this adventure. It includes these three stanzas:

> We have eased ourselves down,
> Promoted the cliff-stairs to safe passage
> Above the sea-howl, each step
> Widening on to the outcrop of armoured rock
> Makes its individual sound as the sea-plants crack
> 'Beach the bloody crates!'
>
> Orders is orders
> For he is no crazy man: pots are expensive
> A living must be got.
> His anger swings in the storm, like a metal moon
> No caution allowed
> In these recondite surroundings.
>
> It was fighting for hours, it seemed
> The wet ropes rasping already frozen fingers
> Till crowding back on the baize shelves of Kilbaha

The crates are counted – six. All safe
He is exultant. The ocean swell behind us,
We'll go to Kilrush and later cash the cheque.

But when finally the big movies stopped coming, I really felt the pinch. Although films dribbled on into the seventies, with movies like John Boorman's *Excalibur*, gradually Ireland became too expensive – hotels and suchlike pricing the companies out. So they moved away to cheaper countries like Spain and Portugal and Greece. The very last job I got was in *Educating Rita*, but only for one day!

But to go back to Finton? Where had he come from? His father had come over during the First World War to avoid conscription. He came from a middle-class family in Edinburgh; by an extraordinary coincidence, Graham McLachlan, my short-lived lover from Kilquhanity School, was his father's nephew. A strange circle in which to be enmeshed. Finton's father was a portrait painter, not all that bad: his portrait of Edward Martin, Yeats's friend, hangs in the National Gallery.

So this man, Norman McLachlan, grimly Presbyterian, arrived in Ireland and married a good Catholic girl from the north-west. They had four sons and three daughters. An awkward man, he fell out with his sitters, refusing to flatter them, so they lived in penury up a boreen in County Wicklow. Subsequently, they moved to the top of Lincoln Place, where they got a flat on a ninety-nine-year lease. He started making furniture, and Finton was taken out of school. According to a report, he was 'an intelligent scholar'.

So after this, it was downhill all the way. The other siblings pulled themselves up by their bootstraps. By getting jobs, they put themselves through college. But Finton, the tearaway, saw petty crime as a more congenial way of making a few bob, and he had the chip of not having been to Trinity firmly latched on to his shoulder.

It is said that he was the favourite, his father taking him everywhere on the back of the bike. So this position in the family enforced his natural belief that he was the centre of an unyielding universe.

Was his father mad always, or did he become mad through adverse circumstances? He turned Catholic, returned to Presbyterianism, and became Catholic again. It is generally believed that he was a schizophrenic and was unable to get a purchase on Irish mores. Eventually, after going in and out of mental institutions, he antagonised his whole family. Finton's sister said later that to have survived their father's cruelty and irrational behaviour was nothing short of a miracle.

I wasn't let meet his parents, although by a sort of osmosis I knew that his father followed us when we went to Stephen's Green. There he was, no mistaking it, hiding in the bushes, staring at us, in particular his grandchildren. Finton never explained why he did not want me to meet his father or mother. I would like to have gone up to the old man and shaken his hand, but I didn't want to scare him.

There were many reasons why Finton felt that he couldn't introduce his family to his parents. He wasn't married to a good Catholic girl – his mother was an ardent churchgoer – and wasn't even married. But mostly, I suspected, it was because I wasn't a beautiful young aristocratic blonde!

In this way, he probably thought he could compartmentalise his life, as, in a similar way, I myself did. Living in Dublin in the sixties, it was often necessary to do this if one was to get any peace of mind. And no one can be blamed for this.

DEATH

Robert McBryde sang for his drinks in McDaid's. 'Wine from the Wood'.

McDaid's was an extraordinary pub. Paddy O'Brien must have been one of the most outstanding barmen of all times. He enjoyed this mélange of artists and writers and hangers-on, while at the same time maintaining order and acting as bank and nursemaid to all and sundry. No, there was no one like Paddy O'Brien. He could pull pints and tease his customers and slap the till with a rhythmic thump – a musician behind the bar who orchestrated an extraordinary era.

The small alcove at the side entrance was christened 'the intensive-care unit'. This was where people huddled off their terminal hangovers, shaking pints in hand. I rarely ventured into the pub during the day because of the children, but when I had the chance, there seemed to be a special atmosphere at those lunchtime sessions. The metabolic graph seems to soar at double the normal speed after the first morning pint, and this made for a buzz of intellectual wit and hilarity.

So McBryde, with his songs and sorrow, joined these soldiers of fortune. He had one shirt and a pair of navy-blue shot-silk trousers. These he washed and ironed every day. A courteous and thoughtful guest and, as I've said, attached to Johnny. He was always talking to him, encouraging him to walk – which

John was reluctant to do. The child was much more interested in playing music. Walking, he thought, was a waste of effort.

Just after John's second birthday, about midnight, there came a knock on the door. It was a Guard, to say that a man was in Vincent's Hospital (then at the bottom of Leeson Street), with a card with this address on it. Did he live there? Finton, who had just come in, went down to the hospital and found McBryde in a coma but still alive. He had been hit by a car as he weaved across the road on his way back from the pub. As Finton stood there, Robert died.

Money had to be collected to get him back to Maybole in Scotland, where his family was. The hat went round, and eventually Tony Cronin and a couple of others accompanied the coffin on the plane. As the plane took off, there was thunder and lightning. People smiled. Perhaps the two Roberts were having their first row in heaven!

He was waked in Dwyer's pub at the bottom of Leeson Street, and a few friends trickled up from London for the funeral. Macdara Woods and his then wife, Letti, were among them.

His itinerant life was over.

For a while afterwards, Johnny looked for him. He missed him. 'Robert Sky,' he used to say in mournful tones. 'Robert Sky.'

ILLNESS

By 1967, I had finished the first draft of the novel *Girl on a Bicycle*. Within these cluttered hours, I found time, when the children were in bed, to sit down at the typewriter. There was always the hope that selling a novel might improve the finances. Also, it was 'there' to write.

Tim O'Keeffe, who was working in the English publishing house McGibbon & Kee, read it and liked it. Hopes rose – to be immediately dashed. Just then, McGibbon & Kee were being amalgamated, and Tim was leaving. He said that without his promotion, the novel would die on its feet. I put it away.

But around this time, Michael Smith had started the New Writers' Press. He came down to the basement and said he'd like to publish a collection of my poems. This resulted in my first collection, *The Mad Cyclist*, which came out in 1970.

At the time, however, I was in a very deep state of anxiety over my son John. I knew he wasn't well: he was far too thin and had a constantly upset stomach. One day, he was eating some strawberries and he brought them up. It was as though a red flag had been raised. I immediately took him into Outpatients in Baggot Street Hospital. On seeing him, the doctor said: 'We'd better take him in.'

'Now?'

'Yes, now.'

Once again, I had to watch one of my babies being led off into hospital. With the incommunicativeness of his tribe, the doctor brushed aside my questions. That evening I went to see John. He was in a small ward with three other children of varying ages. Naturally he didn't like being there, but he was warm and clean and I tried not to worry. After a few days, having visited him twice a day, I finally tracked down an intern. He told me that John was suspected of being a coeliac. Again he wouldn't elucidate. Up till now, of course, I had imagined the worst possible condition, and in my fearful state of confusion and anxiety I sought out medical books, pacing the streets alone, not knowing where to turn. Through reading, I discovered the cause of the condition. I went up to the same intern again. Bland and dismissive, he told me to stop reading books. *One must not interfere with the great medical mind. Mothers, especially, have small brains and should not bother their pretty heads with something they can't understand.* Frustrated and furious, I was up against a bureaucratic wall. John lost more weight, and became too weak to get up even, but because of his extraordinary intellect, he maintained a high level of conversation.

Just then, Billy and Dave visited. They were to go for a picnic. Finton threw me out of the car. 'Get washed,' he ordered. 'You're not coming like that.' I had no interest in my appearance. I was dirty and not fit company for anyone.

But then, a miracle happened. My Uncle Bob, the paediatrician, home on holiday from Nigeria, visited me. I begged him to do something. I told him of John's illness, that the hospital didn't seem to be doing anything, and if anything the child was getting weaker and weaker.

All hell broke loose. Bob had worked with coeliacs and knew immediately what should be done. As he said later, this is one of the simplest conditions to diagnose, and the child should have been sent home ages before and put on a gluten-free diet. As

John said afterwards: 'Before, I had no doctors. Now I have three!' He also said: 'I'm not staying here another minute!' So out he came – to my enormous relief – and straightway I put him on the correct foods.

I have often given out about my Uncle Bob Collis, for always wanting to be in control, but I will never forget how intelligent and immediate his reaction was when I told him of John's condition. One could indeed say that he saved his life. (When I write these words, I get a repetition of that knot of fear lodging in my stomach.)

It was an awful experience for the child. But once he was home, his appetite returned and he slowly put on weight.

More Deaths and Endings

The parties in Leeson Street were winding down. A couple called McNeice – Miriam and Paddy – had moved into 1 Hatch Place, next door to Patsy Murphy. Paddy was a junior maths lecturer in UCD. People began to gather there after the pubs. The same crowd simply shifted over.

However, there was still a constant stream of visitors to No. 33, during the day. Endless cups of tea, problems being sifted, unravelled and momentarily set aside. Macdara Woods and Paul Durcan were daily guests, and Paul introduced us to the songs of Bob Dylan, with whom we afterwards became besotted. And Macdara's sister Orla, and her friend Bernie. Also Patsy Murphy, who lived next door to the McNeices in Hatch Place. And these young women were a godsend. Days alone with babies are long. And it was during this time that I had the good fortune to see more of the poet Eiléan Ní Chuilleanáin.

But the couple, Paddy and Miriam, who seemed so normal and settled on the surface, were anything but, underneath. Paddy, a handsome, speedy young man, with one of those lean, inquisitive faces, suffered from a kind of depression. It is possible that he saw himself following on the heels of older lecturers, becoming dependent on alcohol, repeating the dreary round day after day. Already he was drinking too heavily, and when he hit the whiskey, he'd get into rows, which sometimes ended in fistfights. During one fracas, he was knocked down, and he hit the back of his head on the pavement, cracking his skull. He was told to cut out the spirits. But he paid no heed.

A few weeks after this, the crowd, having thinned out, left John Jordan on the sofa talking to Miriam.

Where was Paddy, they wondered?

What happened after this is too awful to imagine. Paddy was hanging from the trapdoor into the attic. Miriam's husband, Paddy McNeice, had taken his life, killed himself quietly and secretly, while Miriam chatted to John in the sitting room below.

Impossible to describe the awesomeness of this happening. Miriam's despair and hopelessness, her effort to come to terms with the tragedy, as it reverberated amongst the people who knew them. John Jordan, in particular, was confused and shattered by having been there. And there were those who truly loved this man, who cared personally for him, whose grief could not be shared.

Some days later, his body was taken to Limerick and buried in the family plot.

The parties were over.

And Then Christopher

So what of all those highs and lows, the laughter, the hilarity, the broken bones, the tragic, unnecessary deaths? What were they all for? Was it love? Or a natural progression through life, searching for the meaning of this four-letter word? I ask this because Christopher came back into my life just then – but for the briefest moment.

As I've said, the parties were over, but one evening, while Dickie Riordan was in the basement, a word had come to me that Christopher was in town, staying at Buswell's Hotel. I do not remember how I found out – searching my memory is too traumatic – but I do remember telling Dickie that I had to go out. He said he would babysit. I said I wouldn't be long. Without putting on my coat, I raced down to Molesworth Street. At the desk: 'Yes, a Christopher Cooper is in Room 26.' I ran up the stairs, and there he was, in bed. His long, emaciated frame emanating his unchangeable good humour. I was surprised – piqued, in fact – that he hadn't sought me out when he was in Ireland, as he had always done in London. Later I found out that he was too ill, his body doubled up with rheumatoid arthritis and God knows what else. What had life doled out to him apart from his scholarship, his zest for living, his sense of humour? I do not know. Selfish and stupid as I was, I thought of him always in relation to myself, having no notion of what had happened to him in the years before my birth and after – years through which we had shared related genes. Yet somehow or other I knew him to be an extraordinary person. For every one, I suppose, there is one other person who stands alone, and for which there can perhaps be no explanation. All I know is that that short time I sat on the chair in the hotel room, the vision of him on the bed, and myself beneath his trenchant stare, the hard brocaded seat, my green Italian jumper, his silk dressing gown, a puddle on the floor, the reading lamp aslant on his book, has become like a cartoon of anamnesis that can never be erased.

His first remarks, before I'd even sat down, were: 'You are not looking as badly as they said.' This remark, like that time long ago when he'd asked me why I had gone back to Cambridge, left me quite disconsolate, like a homeless person, who has long ago run out of excuses for their derelict condition. I knew then that he had discussed me, probably with his cousin Patsy Cooper. What had they said? That I was wrecking my life with an impossible man? Who knows? I didn't query it. I tried to persuade him to get up and come back up to Leeson Street. But he had taken a sleeping pill.

I was tongue-tied. I could have asked him so many things. But no, I was over-ebullient, unable to cope with my equivocal emotions. I wanted to tell him that I was fine, getting poems published, coping, but I told him none of this. I sat, on that hard chair beside his bed, like a pathetic waif. I went out and down the stairs. I would never see him again.

The Last of Leeson Street

As I've said, my twins, Billy and Anna, always came over in the holidays, maybe for a week or ten days. This was never really satisfactory on either side. For them, they had to slot into my chaotic lifestyle, and I could never give them the time they needed, although I always tried to organise excursions to the hills with them. It was complex, and for me sometimes heart-scalding, especially seeing them off each time, watching them go through the barrier on to the mailboat: that pain behind the eyes!

When Jacky used to go to Brian in England, I missed her terribly. She was such a good friend, and a buttress against the whirlwind of difficulties, both human and financial, with which I daily had to cope. And of course a constant help with her younger brothers.

As I have said, she was obsessed with dancing and had trained in the Ballet Rambert. Now, in Dublin, she enrolled in the Dun Laoghaire Ballet School, and worked as a model in the Dublin Art College to pay for her fees.

Her heart wasn't in her school lessons, so when she had finished her Inter Cert, she decided to take the boat to England. She had been in many performances, in the Olympia and the Players Wills Theatre, but she felt that she was getting nowhere with the Dun Laoghaire company.

It was devastating for me when she left, but she had to make her own decision. Her childhood in Leeson Street, advantageous in some ways, was also lonely and hard. Because of my selfishness and inability to stay still, the onus of childminding all too often fell on her shoulders. But selfishly, I'm glad I had at least one daughter to keep me company during those lean years.

But before this, in 1967, Kavanagh, who had suffered a bout of pneumonia, was very low in health. Katherine was over on holiday, and Paddy said he could no longer live in Ireland without her. She must find a job in Dublin. They would marry.

She got a job ('One of us has to have a job, Paddy told her!'), and they moved into a flat in Fitzwilliam Place.

Paddy loved his wedding. He said that he had never been happier. It was a great event, and hit the headlines. But unfortunately he was not well. Ever since his lung operation in the fifties, he had been prone to pneumonia. He dragged around for months but was not able to withstand the winter. On 30 November of that year, he died. (The same day as my son Nicholas's birthday, about which years later he wrote a fine poem.)

There was a tremendous funeral in Iniskeen, and the miserable village that had despised him all his life had to sit up and take notice. The owner of McNello's pub said at the funeral: 'And the aul' fucker owed me five pounds!'

Just before his death, he had been awarded £1,000 by the British Arts Council. Too late.

The headlines in the *Irish Times*: 'THE POET PATRICK KAVANAGH DIES'. Yes, it was too late.

That era was closing down. Myles na gCopaleen had died the year before, and Brendan Behan.

I had not known either of them. Myles was very bitter – and rightly so – about his novels, having been turned down by various publishers. And Behan, by then always seen with his legmen

— thug-like individuals — did not endear himself to the majority in McDaid's.

You could say that with the end of the sixties, 'La Vie de Bohème' ended. Luckily, perhaps.

Writers, artists and composers do not self-destruct in the same way any more — or at least it's rare.

In 1969, our landlord gave us notice to quit. And on 1 August 1970, we moved into 1 Hatch Place.

The angels had folded their wings.